MIDDLESEX VOL II

Edited by Lynsey Hawkins

First published in Great Britain in 2003 by
YOUNG WRITERS
Remus House,
Coltsfoot Drive,
Peterborough, PE2 9JX
Telephone (01733) 890066

HB ISBN 1 84460 156 0
SB ISBN 1 84460 157 9

FOREWORD

Young Writers was established in 1991 as a foundation for promoting the reading and writing of poetry amongst children and young adults. Today it continues this quest and proceeds to nurture and guide the writing talents of today's youth.

From this year's competition Young Writers is proud to present a showcase of the best poetic talent from across the UK. Each hand-picked poem has been carefully chosen from over 66,000 'Hullabaloo!' entries to be published in this, our eleventh primary school series.

This year in particular we have been wholeheartedly impressed with the quality of entries received. The thought, effort, imagination and hard work put into each poem impressed us all and once again the task of editing was a difficult but enjoyable experience.

We hope you are as pleased as we are with the final selection and that you and your family will continue to be entertained with *Hullabaloo! Middlesex Vol II* for many years to come.

CONTENTS

Buxlow Preparatory School

Colham Manor Primary School

Coteford Junior School

Charlotte Gailey	58
Amy Ward	58
Jasmeet Matharu	59
Sarah Gratton	59
Ross Allen	60
Shelbie Franks	60
Daniel Parry	61
Alex Davis	61
Zoe Edwards	62
Rebecca Dalglish	62
Luke O'Brien	63
James Ketteridge	63
Tamar Ayres	64
Hannah Victoria Monk	64
Simren Degun	65
Yanil Patel	65
Daniel Harrington	66
Alexandra Shaw	67
Zoe Huggett	68
Isabel Foley	68
Sophie Harris-Edmond	69
Lauren Currivan	69
Christopher Arnold	70
Ruth Sarah Barclay	71
Charlotte James	72
Helen Scibilia	73
Muhaddisa Datoo	74
Rebecca Hanington	74
Matthew Gleeson	75
Rhys Bradbury	75
Elliott Coghill	76
Kristina Greally	77
Jade Short	78
Helen Townsend	78
Rebecca Smith	79
Joe Griffiths	79
Jade Spires	80
Kathryn Sansby	80

Max Pendry	81
Bhadrika Parmar	81
Leah Davies	82
Sanam Batavia	82
Arik Rubens	83
Dominique Lawrence	83
Kavil Patel	84
Shiv Kharbanda	84
Ashleigh Coombs	85
Frances Millman	86
Becky Robinson	87
Louis Monckton	88
Matthew Harris	88
Fleur Harman	88
Jessica Henderson	89
Chris Hills	89
Charlie May	90
Gavin Barclay	91
Amy Kenny	92
Kerry Stack	92
William Pearmain	93
Martin James	94
Benjamin Shaw	95
Khiszer Butt	96

Hambrough Primary School

Mariam Jussab	96
Aileen Suresh	97
Sunil Mair	97
Pratichi Vaghela	98
Hardeep Bharj	98
Asha Jimale	99
Gurpreet Matharou	100
Vinood Saroop	100
Nikesh Gohil	101
Ayat Mansab	102
Reshma Sharma	102
Iqra Bhatti	103

Amarjit Chana	104
Simran Gill	104
Kimrit Marway	104
Vishal Ehounhan	105
Geerthana Vigneswaran	105
Karishma Fatania	106
Vanisha Bharadwa	106

Hayes Park Primary School

Nia Acquaye	107
Hayley Brimble	107
Abby Stokes	108
Bhavinder Reyatt	108
Daniel Dyer	108
Nicholas Everley	109
David Walker	109
Daniel Rickwood	109
Alice Rose Shilling	110
Hannah Seers	110
Francesca Browne	111
Max Corner	111
Ifrah Rafique Nasseem	112
Sian Forbes-White	112
Jake Louis Pulman	113
Rahul Nisanth	113
Jaskiran Virdee	114
Michaela Pearce	114
Josh Leighton	115
Bradley Clarke	115
Jordan Berry	116
Lauren Mason	116
Annie Jones	116
Dylan Saib	117
Harlie Shelton	117
Charlotte Fairclough	118
Karan Soni	118
Olivia Carpenter	119
Krish Pattni	119

Tudor Primary School

The Poems

THERE WAS A CAT THAT WAS VERY FAT

There was a cat that was very fat.
There was a dog that was as brown as a log.
There was a bug that had its own mug.
There was a man with a fan.
There was a snake around a cake.
There was a cow that loved to plough.
There was a hen who had a precious pen.
And that's the end of my poem my friend.

Nalin Chadha (8)

MY LITTLE CANDLE

My little candle glows so bright
It is my only light
When I look closely it makes be blink
My mind starts to think
It makes me wonder who I am and why am I here
People begin to look
Then start to stare
I cover my face with my maths book
The laughing starts
My head is in a spin
I throw my candle in the bin
The laughing stops
My maths book drops
That little light has gone
And so has the damage that the laughter has done.

Lauren Dodd (12)
Aylward First & Middle School

OUR FAIRY QUEEN

To keep our fairy queen safe,
You're never to see a frown on her face!

That's why I've come up with this spell,
Which will keep her smiling and well.

A few bits and bobs all mixed up,
Now all we need is a very large cup

And a spoon to stir, stir, stir,
That's when strange things begin to occur!

Now all we need is:-

A human's hair like a golden wire,
As fierce as coal of red-hot fire.

Then when a hedgehog finally does appear,
Take its prickle that's as sharp as a spear.

When all the humans are asleep,
Pass them we slowly creep.

Through the town and silent streets,
Where it's deserted, no one meets.

Through the slushy mud we pass,
Collecting all the yellow grass!

We went to get some dirty water but as we did,
We saw humans so we hid!

We tiptoed past him hoping not to be seen,
In the reflection of the water stream!

So don't come near our fairy queen,
Where the creepy insects hide when they're seen!

Energetic frogs and slow snails
Leave the slimy prints and trails

If our queen was hurt by a boy or girl,
Hell! Then we would cast this spell!

Georgina Lilley (11)
Aylward First & Middle School

CANDLES

The flame of a candle grows with pleasure,
I will treasure that flame for ever and ever.

That flame that burns so hot, so bright,
So dazzling and full of delight.

Light me, light me, let me shine,
Show my family that I am divine.

Candle, candle, burning low,
Flickering, flickering to and fro.

Jade Moore (11)
Aylward First & Middle School

THE CANDLES

The light of the candles flickered in the wind,
It brightened up the room,
It made the evil darkness blind
And called the light of Heaven.

Johann Nelson (11)
Aylward First & Middle School

CANDLELIGHT
(In the style of Blake)

Candle, candle! Burning bright
Piercing through the darkened night.

Flickering, flickering! Burning low,
Waving in the wind as it blows.

Candle, candle! Burning bright,
Piercing through the darkened night.

Jeanine Ellington (12)
Aylward First & Middle School

CANDLES

Beautiful ring with candles burning bright,
Five candles brighten your sight.
One pretty candle, every Sunday,
Watch them burn while you play.
Four candles, red they will be,
One white candle for Christmas,
For you and for me.

Alice Jennings (11)
Aylward First & Middle School

AN ANGEL

An angel appeared in a golden shroud,
The feathers on her wings fluttered out proud.
Her halo shone out bright and gold,
A beautiful sight to behold.

Her voice rang out sweet and mild,
To tell us of a newborn child.
The angel's trumpet sounded loud and clear,
Jesus Christ at last was here.

Katie Shephard (11)
Aylward First & Middle School

FOUR LITTLE CANDLES

Four little candles all have a flame,
One shall black out and he has the blame
And when they flicker it's like a game,
Four little candles all have a glow,
Four little candles go out with one blow.

Brett Madigan (11)
Aylward First & Middle School

CANDLE POEM

Burning so bright,
You are my only light,
Your shimmering shine,
Stands in line,
So strong and tall,
Never do you fall,
Your flickering fire
Is my only desire,
My eternal flame.

Jessica Barry (11)
Aylward First & Middle School

The Light Of The Night

I looked into the night,
Saw a candle burning bright,
Banishing the night to light,
The light's might defeating the night,
I looked into the night.

Eli Pearson (11)
Aylward First & Middle School

My Weird Family

My cousin Jacko is really wacko
My auntie Kerry is really hairy
My uncle Paul is really tall
    That's my family

My cousin Jean is really mean
My auntie Sue always uses the loo
My uncle Pete has smelly feet
    That's my family

My cousin Tony is really bony
My auntie Kat loves to chat
My uncle Dan thinks he's the man
    That's my family

My cousin Shawn loves to eat corn,
My auntie Lin always sits near the bin,
My uncle Tim is really slim
    That's my family!

Maria Derissy (10)
Barham Primary School

AM I OLD?

Little laddie, come over here,
Look into my eyes,
What do you see?
A stubborn old man or a boy under a tree?
I have been waiting for the answer day and night,
Please tell me now!
I am dying to know,
It is just the words 'Yes' or 'No'
I am walking to and fro across the hall,
Tell me, before I fall,
Do you understand the pain I feel?
'Yes' or 'No' is the way to heal,
Take a deep breath and answer me,
Am I old or am I just me?

Anujah Sachchithanantham (10)
Barham Primary School

IT'S NOT THE SAME

It's not the same since Amie left,
Her smiling face has turned to dust,
Her funny jokes last no more,
It's not the same.

No more funny faces,
No more laughter from her face.

When Amie left,
She's like my best friend,
But it never lasts.

Monica Patel (9)
Barham Primary School

MY WAY THROUGH THE WOODS

As I walk through the woods at night,
I'm glad for the glory of the moonlight.
As I look above me,
The trees form a canopy.
Tree after tree, all standing tall,
Sheltering me from the heavy rainfall.
The owl flies by,
I see its glowing white eyes.
The owl on the tree is my instigator,
Warning me about the nearby danger,
Telling me about the dreaded creepy crawler,
On top of that, the forest monster.
Green, black, brown and white,
My inner fright is taken away from the whole so bright.
Finally reality strikes me
And now it's the end of my difficulty.

Bhavik Gami (11)
Barham Primary School

IT'S NOT THE SAME ANYMORE

It's not the same since Amie left
Her kindness and her letting people play with her
The sole gatekeeper of peace and friendship
Her great sportsmanship and talent for playing games
Especially cricket

Without her, school has changed
She used to bring laughter to even the
Saddest of people and never gave up on a challenge
She tried her hardest in everything.

Yashvant Nandha (10)
Barham Primary School

VOICES OF THE WATER

The water in the jungle says
'Come to me!'

Splish, splash, sip, trip, splash!

The water in the sea goes *whoosh, whoosh!*
The water in the bath goes *rash, rish.*
The water in the sink says clean me!
With the plates, *sh, sh.*

The water in the stream says *whoosh, whoosh!*
The water in your glass says *plan, plur!*
The water in your stomach goes *gur, gur!*
The water in the bubbles go *plop, plop!*
The water in my kettle goes *shu, shu!*
The water in your teacup goes *pur, pur!*

Vandana Patel (10)
Barham Primary School

IT'S NOT THE SAME SINCE HANNAH LEFT

It's not the same since Hannah left,
Her smiling face has turned to dust,
Oh! Hannah please come back to us!

It's not the same since Hannah left,
Our happiness has drowned away,
Oh! Hannah please come back to us!

It's not the same since Hannah left,
Our friendship has sank to the bottom of the sea,
Oh! Hannah please come back to us!

Dinusha Fernando, Zoe Lee & Milly Mehta (10)
Barham Primary School

MY WAY THROUGH THE WOODS

The way through the woods at midnight,
Scared to death at midnight.

The moon's light, not too bright
What shall I do in the middle of the night?

The way through the woods, creepy and scary,
The trees laughing at me while I run on and on.

The grass shivering and scaring me,
The animals' eyes creeping me out.

The tree so tall, bending down,
Midnight begins. What shall I do?

Maira Majid (10)
Barham Primary School

POEMS

Machines, machines,
Machines, machines,
Everywhere, everywhere, even in dreams.
Tickaty, tack, tickaty, tack,
Machines, machines, *crick, crack,*
Drip, drop, drip, drop,
Splash, splash, splish, splash,
Listen to machines *crish, crash.*

Clanging, clanging, banging, banging,
Zigzag, splash, splash,
Machines, machines, oh my gosh,
I cannot stand them,
Wash, wash, splish, splosh.

Ramsha Qadri (10)
Barham Primary School

IMAGINE

Imagine if bricks fell from the sky
And trees grew below,
If it's really raining cats and dogs
And there's no such thing as Big Bro's nu flow.

Imagine if birds couldn't fly, but we can as well
And if the sea was sand
And instead of arms, we had wings
And we only had one hand.

Imagine if we had school at night
And we could play all day,
If we could stay in the playground,
Hey, hey, hey, hip, hip, hooray!

So if this was really true,
The teachers would be sued,
This could be fun,
But hey, run, run, run, run,
For it's raining cats and dogs
And bricks are falling from the sky
And all the teachers did their tricks.

Elizabeth Domingo Mercado (11)
Barham Primary School

FAMILY PROBLEMS

I have a strange uncle called Kenny
He's small and squashed like a penny
On cold winter days
When standing in the way
You can tell he's had one too many.

Nafisah Kara (11)
Barham Primary School

MY DOG, ROCKY

It's not the same
Since my Rocky left

I miss his barking
I miss his dribbling
I miss the ball rolling
Outside the patio

I miss my dog a lot

I cried
I spoke
I've thought about my dog
Ever since he left
Please come back!

Navraj Hunjan (10)
Barham Primary School

MY FAMILY

My family is completely insane,
In fact I'm the only one that's not,
My brother is always a pain
And my sister, well, she's just lost the plot.

My dad just lost his job,
My mum's afraid of mice,
My cousins hate corn on the cob
And my grandparents are nuts about rice!

Kalpana Gorasia (11)
Barham Primary School

FRIENDSHIP

You're . . .
My friend,
My companion,
Through good times and bad,
My friend,
My buddy,
Through happy and sad.
Beside me you stand,
Beside me you walk,
You're there to listen,
You're there to talk,
With happiness,
With smiles,
With pain and tears,
I know you'll be there,
Throughout the years.

Mariam Bhandari (10)
Barham Primary School

THE WATER IN THE RIVER SAYS

The water in the river says
Drip, drip, hush, hush.
The water in the sea says
Crash, crash, trill, trill.
The water in the pond says,
Plosh, plosh, rish, rish.
The water in the ocean says,
Sip, sip, trip, trip.

Pooja Patel (10)
Barham Primary School

IN THE WOODS

When the night air cools on the trout
Ringed pools
The old lost road through the woods . . .
(They fear not men in the woods,
Because they see so few)
Yet, if you enter the woods
Where the otter whistles his mate
And the steady swish of a skirt in the dew,
As though they perfectly knew
But there is no way through the woods
And the badgers roll at ease
Seventy years ago.
That, where the ring-dove broods,
Before they planted the trees
Of a summer evening late,
The misty solitudes,
Weather and rain have undone it again,
Only the keeper sees
Steadily cantering through
And now you would never know
There was once a road through the woods.

Carita Bellot (10)
Barham Primary School

ORANGE, OH ORANGE

Orange, oh orange,
You're so orange,
I wonder where you came from,
Orange, oh orange,
You're so tasty,
There's no room now for chocolate.

Sharjeel Kiani (11)
Barham Primary School

MY FAVOURITE BROTHER

I have a brother,
Who is very fat.
His belly is like jelly.
His nose is in the telly.
His eyes are all red
And his favourite food is bread.
His ears covered with a hat
And his nose is dripping and flat.
He loves to make bets
With his best friend's pets.
My brother is quite lazy
And he is a bit crazy.
I love my brother
And he is really *good,*
When he's not in a *mood!*

Amar Jani (11)
Barham Primary School

TEACHERS, WHAT DO YOU EXPECT?

Drinking and driving
Throwing tins and breaking bins
Thinking with their toes
Lucky that it glows
And that's the way it shows
It shows some nasty toes
Embarrassed and scared
They decided to pose.

Nevine Amer (10)
Barham Primary School

MY MAGIC BOX
(Based on 'Magic Box' by Kit Wright)

I will put in the box
My family's love so I do not lose it
I will put in the box
My friendship to keep forever
I will put in the box
The birds' songs to hear every day
I will put in the box
Cruel people that are cruel to nature
I will put in the box
Some gold and silver to keep everybody happy
I will put in the box
My first birthday card for memories
I will put in the box
My first present from my mum so I will remember her
Then I will shut it.

Keshini Patel (9)
Buxlow Preparatory School

SCHOOL CHAOS

One day in school
Chaos struck!
Screaming, shouting
No one stopped
The lights went off
The door was shut
Everyone kept screaming
It got worse
The fire alarm went off
They all got out
But one was lost.

Annabel Mizel (9)
Buxlow Preparatory School

CLASSROOM CHATTER

As soon as the teacher left the room
The hullabaloo was enormous
There were laughs and cries
There were shrieks and yells
And this went on for quite a while
But as soon as the teacher came back
It all stopped as though it had never begun

Also in class when the teacher was in,
It did keep on going but with much less din
If the teacher saw the person who made the hullabaloo
Zip, out the door they go.

Davy Cruickshank (9)
Buxlow Preparatory School

THE FLU

When my brother had the flu,
There was such a racket and hullabaloo.
He went to bed and was feeling blue,
His nose was red and ticklish too,
He coughed and sneezed and then went,
Atishoo!
Mum was furious and shouted,
'What is all this hullabaloo?'
When he was better,
My mum began to chatter.
No more cold, no more flu,
Playing now, my brother still makes a
Hullabaloo.

Soraya McGinley (9)
Buxlow Preparatory School

LET'S CELEBRATE

I celebrate
Knowing my family cares about me
Having such kind and lovely friends to play with
That even for no reason I get a little surprise
Whenever I'm ill
Just a smile from my mum or dad makes me feel better
Even sometimes when my parents
Can't help me
My brother or sister does
But most of all
I love seeing my family together
Because
That's how I celebrate.

Sophia Kleanthous (9)
Buxlow Preparatory School

HULLABALOO IN A THESAURUS

Hullabaloo is a lion roaring,
Hullabaloo is a teacher shouting,
Hullabaloo is a rocket taking off,
Hullabaloo is a digger digging,
Hullabaloo is a bomb exploding,
Hullabaloo is a tree falling,
Hullabaloo is glass breaking,
Hullabaloo is steam blowing,
Hullabaloo is a horse calling,
Hullabaloo is a car crashing,
Hullabaloo is a toy breaking,
Snap! The thesaurus closes!

Alok Prinja (9)
Buxlow Preparatory School

How To Stay Awake In Class

Play with your ruler, reflecting many a shape,
Go ahead and daydream about a great escape.
Drink coffee in the morning but make sure that nobody knows,
Or busy yourself sticking pens up your nose.

Nibble your pencil until it's almost gone,
Or pen notes until you go home and the lights are not on,
Go and jump up and down but you'll get into trouble,
But the teacher shouting could just burst your bubble.

Play around until it is break,
Then I'm sure you'll be awake,
Or you could just listen to the teacher.

Barath Nair (9)
Buxlow Preparatory School

Hullabaloo

H avoc in the classroom, children everywhere;
U nder the tables, you name it, they were there.
L oads of laughter, panic in the air,
L ots of shouting, here and there.
A ll around were books and toys;
B ig and small, girls and boys.
A t last 'twas home time although no one seemed to moan,
L ost was the teacher, suddenly left alone.
O h what a day, she quietly said,
O h how I wish that for the rest of my life,
                I could lie alone in bed!

Nimlan Shanmugathas (11)
Buxlow Preparatory School

THE MAGIC BOX
(Based on 'Magic Box' by Kit Wright)

I will put in my box . . .
All the friendship and laughter
To listen to when I'm sad
I will put in my box . . .
My special toy teddy
That I was given when I was born
To cuddle when I'm lonely
I will put in my box . . .
All the imaginary things
I have longed for since I was small
I will put in my box . . .
Animals, safe from poachers,
That I will protect forever
I will put in my box . . .
The secret of joy and fun
So that I can always give some
To people who are miserable
I will put in my box . . .
My imaginary, peaceful world
That I hope one day will be one we live in
All I have to do is
Open the box
Put something inside
Shut the box tight
And keep it where I only know.

Komal Shah (10)
Buxlow Preparatory School

LET'S CELEBRATE

Let's celebrate the fact that we have no starvation,
Where other countries do.
They have no food or any clear water,
Just imagine how they might feel.

Let's celebrate the fact that we live near no wars,
Where other countries suffer.
They have no rights,
Just imagine how they might be put through torture.

Let's celebrate the fact that we have good education,
Where other countries do not.
They have no schools or anything of such,
Just imagine the way they might live.

Let's celebrate the fact that we have good doctors and nurses,
Where other people have to sit through the pain.
They have no help,
Just imagine how they might hurt.

Let's celebrate the fact that we have everything we might need,
Where other people might not,
They have to make toys and things they need,
Just imagine how they occupy their time.

We must be very lucky to have so many things,
So let's be happy and appreciate *everything!*

Priya Thakrar (10)
Buxlow Preparatory School

HULLABALOO

When I woke up in the morning,
I did not have a clue
That at the midnight party,
There would be a hullabaloo.

When I arrived at the party,
Hardly anything went right;
And what was most unpleasant,
Was the heating and the light.

For when everyone was dancing,
The party lights went out.
All the children (boys and girls)
Began to scream and shout.

First there was a commotion;
The adults made it worse.
I just stood there, waiting
For the crowd to disperse.

By 2 o'clock in the morning,
There was a hullabaloo.
I struggled towards the big front door
And managed to get through.

Farhaan Keshani (11)
Buxlow Preparatory School

LET'S CELEBRATE

Let's celebrate the love and care,
We have from our family and friends,
When so many people are alone in this world
And their loved ones have turned against them.
We are lucky to have this friendship and care,

When it's the only thing others want,
With friends standing by our sides we have confidence,
Like no one else has,
So let's celebrate these important things instead
Of wanting more and more.

Olivia Majumdar (9)
Buxlow Preparatory School

THE SEA

The sea is calm with wispy waves and seaweed on the bay.
Beautiful shells lay on the sand with different shades of white and grey.
There's an old jetty that stands by the edge of the sea.

Sometimes I get my deckchair out and sit on the end
Of the jetty with a cup of fruit tea.
I sit there for hours and watch the golden sun go down,
The sea is so clear like a freshly-poured glass of water.
I play with sand and skim stones and I can hear them
Go plop, plop as they sink under the water.

Often you can see the dolphins jump in the air
And hear them make their funny noise.
I dive in the water and I swim deep under
And see all the colourful fish and fascinating animals.
It's all so peaceful and calm; I wish that I could live under the water,
When I move away all I will have left are the beautiful shells
I collected and the photographs and memories.

Lindsay Inglis (10)
Colham Manor Primary School

MY TEACHER

My teacher's name is Mrs Rose
And she's got a very long nose,
She always orders us around
And we cannot make a sound.

When my teacher does not look
I rip a page out of my book,
I write a short note to my mate
Telling her the things I hate.

She taught us lots of maths today
Then we all went out to play,
After lunch we had PE
I asked Laura to run with me.

Her hair is very long and brown
And she always wears it down,
With a clip on either side
Or a very pretty slide.

She's very thin, not fat at all
For lunch she has something quite small,
A sandwich, yoghurt, cup of tea
Sometimes she sits next to me.

She can be very kind to us
One day she took us on a bus,
I like my teacher even though
My friends and I don't let her know.

I'll miss my teacher when I go
Even though she'll never know,
I'll miss the smile she gave us all
Her friendly look is really cool.

Fleur Soodeen (10)
Colham Manor Primary School

MY DAY AT SCHOOL

Assembly every morning,
Yes it is so boring,
Listening all that time,
Are you sure that's fine?

Oh, I bet you can guess,
It's literacy next,
Children work hard whilst
The teacher text.

Yes it's playtime now,
Boys are playing footie,
Girls act like Sooty,
Sorry play time's over now.

It's maths now,
Better switch my brain on,
Time to work with my pal,
Yes, last question, thank God for that!

Whoopee, it's PE now,
We've got a guest,
The game's started, it looks a mess,
But I still think it's the best!

Lunch,
Rumble, rumble goes my stomach,
The crisps go *crunch*,
That's the end of my lunch.

It's almost home time now,
Gotta get my homework,
Then go home and sort out my phone work,
Anyway that's my day at school.

Christie Duhig (10)
Colham Manor Primary School

A Poem About School

Assembly in the morning,
Listening all that time.
How do you do it?
And you say it's fine.

Then it's maths,
Miss Taylor teaches,
She makes us work hard,
While she thinks of beaches.

Then it's play time,
Whoopee!
Now it's even closer to home time and tea.

The bell rings,
People come in,
It's PE now,
The excitement begins.

Running around like lunatics,
I'm afraid handball went in a mix.

Alfie pushed,
Jessica fell,
Hannah stared and then thought she'd tell.

The rest of the day soon went,
It was so uncool,
But anyway that's my day at school.

Claire Woodley (10)
Colham Manor Primary School

ANIMALS I CAN SEE

What I saw at home
Let me tell you what I saw
I saw a butterfly, it was so colourful
I saw a bumblebee, it was so wonderful
I saw a little worm, it wiggled around
I saw a fat bug, it looked like a pound
I saw a tall dinosaur, it was as tall as a house
I saw an ant, it was as small as a mouse
I saw a dog, a big spotted dog
I saw a cat in the cold fog
I saw a bird flying through the sky
I saw a goat watching that bird fly

When I went to the zoo
Let me tell you what I saw
I saw an elephant, as wide as a shed
I saw a nice cow that had only just been fed
I saw a zebra, it had loads of stripes
I saw a pink pig, watching some kits

When I went to a safari park
Let me tell you what I saw
I saw a lion eating pie
I saw a tiger having a race and it was a tie
I saw an elephant, as big as a tree
I saw a giraffe, as tall as can be
I saw a monkey being silly
I saw a horse playing with my friend, Tilly

When I went to the farm
Let me tell you what I saw
I saw a sheep playing with the monkey
I saw a gorilla being funky.

Charlie Cook (8)
Colham Manor Primary School

IN THE CLASSROOM

In the classroom
No one knows but
Our teacher is an alien
I stayed behind school
And I saw the teacher take her mask off
Her face was green and slimy
She had a nose as big as Pinocchio
And teeth as yellow as the sun
The she took her wig off
Then . . . she took her . . . *teeth* out
She went over to my drawer and took my pen and ate it
How disgusting
Then . . . I woke up
And went back
To school and it was true.

Natalie Beale (9)
Colham Manor Primary School

THE SWEET SHOP POEM

We have a sweet shop
A gooey-louie sweet stall
A fab and sweety sweet store

We have a sweet store
A nice and candy sweet shop
A yummy that makes your tummy rumble sweet stall

We have a sweet shop
A colourful sweet stall
A loving and beautiful sweet store.

Beckie Dobson (9)
Colham Manor Primary School

MORE SPACE . . .

I gaze into the dark at night
I wonder, space what are you?
If you do go on forever, where did you start?
When I see a shooting star, where does it go rushing off to?
Space, you are full of weird things
But there is so much space between them!
No gravity but fireballs!
They're so powerful, but I can only see you as a twinkle
Space, you seem like a black curtain
But when I draw you back, there is more space . . .

Christopher Harrison (9)
Coteford Junior School

MY POEM

We had to write a poem
About anything we liked
I sat and thought
My mind went blank
Nothing could I think

I know what
I'll have a drink
That'll help me think
By now my brain was in a muddle
Come here Dad – I think I need a cuddle

I know what, it's coming to me now
Maybe it would be better
If I tried tomorrow.

Lauren Catt (9)
Coteford Junior School

SNOW

Snow has fallen in my street,
Right up past my feet.
Glistening white in the sun,
It really is a lot of fun.
It makes a crunchy, creaky sound,
When my foot touches the ground.
I tell myself to be bold,
When I go out in the cold.
The heat inside beckons to me,
So I go inside and see . . .
Hot chocolate on the table,
I'll drink it when my fingers are able,
To pick it up,
Then I'll slurp it from the cup.
Finally the snow does go,
Goodbye I say, I'll miss you so!

Joanna Blackburn (9)
Coteford Junior School

SO FAR AWAY

(A poem to my stepbrother)

Dale was my stepbrother, close to my heart
I loved him from the very start

It makes me sad when I see his grave
But I know I've got to be brave

I remember the very happy days
We had in December.

Lauren Allcroft (8)
Coteford Junior School

IF I WERE A FISH

Imagine my life as a fish
Swimming around in the sea
Beautiful colours that live down here with me
Oh what a life it will be

Imagine my life as a fish
Eating big, slimy worms
Playing with the others in the sea
Oh what a life it will be

Imagine my life as a fish
Meeting other things
Like dolphins, octopuses, jellyfish and more
Oh what a life it will be

Imagine my life as a fish
With dolphins that splash about
And octopus with his eight wiggly legs
And jellyfish with their poisonous tentacles

Imagine my life as a fish
I could see a shark that chases me about
With its sharp teeth
Oh what a life it will be.

Charlotte Crawford (9)
Coteford Junior School

SNOW

S   now falling from the sky
N   ice warm fire
O   h let's build a snowman
W   arm scarf, hat and gloves.

Alexander Barnes (8)
Coteford Junior School

BEYBLADE BATTLE!

Ready steady, get set, go, launching high in the air!
Swirling, whirling everywhere.

They hit the ground, still whizzing round,
Soon the winner will be found!

Bash, crash, two collide,
One is lying on its side!

Two still turning,
Spinning round, spinning, twisting with no sound.
Speeding on till the winner is found.

They're slowing down now, fading fast,
Which one will be the one to last?

The crowd look on with bated breath,
To see which Beyblade won the test!

Miles Connors (9)
Coteford Junior School

THE SNOWBALL FIGHT

White, thick snow
At last it came
Soft and fluffy
Ready for a game

Snowball fighting
Was about to start
Gloves at the ready
Will play their part

Hats and scarves
Cover their faces
Backwards and forwards
Children take their places

Hits and misses
It's all done
The children stop
They've had so much fun.

Katie Patman (10)
Coteford Junior School

MY FRIEND

Sometimes I find things hard to do,
I'd like to run and jump like you.
Sometimes I fall and bump my head
And my elbows or my knees instead.
You help me up and dust me down
And help to take away my frown.

Some days it's hard to be me,
As I find it hard to see.
You help me out and read the lines,
So my work is done on time.

You are my friend,
I'm glad to say,
You make me happy every day.
Thank you, for being so kind,
A friend like you is hard to find.

Annie Connors (10)
Coteford Junior School

SNOW

Snow can come at Christmas,
Snow can come in autumn,
Snow can come in summer
And even come in spring.

Its flakes fall like angels' tears
And those from misty heavens,
It sparkles and glistens like sugar frosting
And looks like white candyfloss.

Snow floats around like feathers,
Turns mundane into wonderland,
The snow melts like moonlight in sunshine
And swiftly moves on.

Chris Reilly (9)
Coteford Junior School

I LOVE SNOW

Snow falls from the sky,
Soft, white flakes,
Pretty shapes and different sizes,
Feels like velvet as it brushes your face,
Just melts in your hand when you catch it,
Oh I love snow!
When it settles on the ground,
As it crunches under your feet,
Sounds like crisps when you eat,
Oh I love snow!

Caleigh Pearson (9)
Coteford Junior School

NUMBER 1 SISTER

She is the best
Better than all the rest
There is no other
She loves her brother

She walks me once a day
No matter what's in her way
She loves me so much
And so do I love her

If she is in trouble
I'm always there for her
And when I'm in trouble
She's there for me

That's why she is
The number 1 sister for me.

Bradley Chambers (10)
Coteford Junior School

THE WIND

It would pounce -
Like a cat.
Struck like lightning,
A bear angry,
Ready to scare.
A furious dog,
Hunting in the woods.
If you are ever lonely -
The wind is always there.

Rebecca Gailey (9)
Coteford Junior School

GRANNY

A crooked smile, an evil grin,
Saliva hanging from her chin,
Suddenly she grabbed my wrist
And in my ear she loudly hissed,
'I've noticed you've grown nice and fat,
I'll eat you instead of my cat,
Now get inside this big black pot,
Where the water's boiling hot.'
Quick and suddenly she pushed me in,
The water was up to my chin,
Just then the water started to boil
And on me she poured olive oil.
I thought I would become a pie,
But to the rescue came a fly!
It flew straight up my grandma's skirt
And off went the grandma's alert,
She couldn't get the insect out,
So she started to scream and shout,
I got out of the pot and ran,
I had escaped being cooked in a pan!

Helen Lee (10)
Coteford Junior School

SCARY . . .

Scary, scary . . .
Shivers running down my spine,
Under the covers I hide in bed,
A necklace of sweat around my head.

Scary, scary . . .
Dark shadows dancing on the wall behind,
Every creaking stair I've ever heard
Echoes in my mind.

Scary, scary . . .
Someone or something . . . lurks outside my door.
What hideous creature might appear?
Then suddenly . . . a whisper,
'Goodnight dear.'

Michael Raimbach (10)
Coteford Junior School

THE DAY IT SNOWED

I was once in my garden,
I was playing on my slide
And it started to snow,
So I decided to go inside.

The snow looked very deep,
The cars were all white,
All the animals were fast asleep,
I really wanted a snow fight!

Today I was in school,
My hair was very wet,
For I was in the swimming pool,
We had an investigation set.

I went out at play time,
I knew a place that was warm,
I sat on the radiator,
Outside felt like a snowstorm.

At the end of that cold winter day,
I was very tired and cold,
I really wished it was the month of May.

Ammh Harwood (10)
Coteford Junior School

BONFIRE NIGHT

B lazing flames
O pening sky
N ight falling
F lashing fireworks
I ntruding bangs amongst the laughter
R acing rockets across the dazzling sky
E xcited children waving sparklers

N ot long now
I can't wait
G uy Fawkes dissolves in the flames
H allowe'en's gone, a week away
T omorrow is another day.

Lawrence Monk (9)
Coteford Junior School

SCHOOL

Tired teachers working all day
Happy children go out to play
Maths, English, science too
Lunch is here
Can I sit with you?
IT, DT, handwriting now
Time to go home
Up to bed
Read a book
Fill it in
Ready for another day
All over again!

Amy Clifford (9)
Coteford Junior School

MY NAUGHTY LITTLE PUPPY

We have a new little puppy
She is black and white
She is sometimes very naughty
With sharp teeth that bite

She is always very naughty
When it's time to go to sleep
She starts to bark loudly
Then she bites my feet

I get up in the morning
She always wants to play
She gets my shoes and my socks
Then she runs away

With my naughty little puppy
I never ever feel sad
Because my naughty little puppy
Is the best friend I have ever had.

Jordan Tuffin (8)
Coteford Junior School

RAIN

Drip, drop, drip
Goes the rain bouncing off my windowpane,
I sit inside by the fire drinking cocoa to my desire.

I sit and gaze out at the street, warm and cosy in my seat,
The clouds have parted and to all my glee,
There is a rainbow for all to see.

Sam Wills (11)
Coteford Junior School

WAS IT A DREAM?

I hear a creak on the stair,
I get up from my sheets,
I open the door
And what do I see there?
I see a creature gazing at me,
Oh, why wasn't I warned?

The creature wears a hooded cloak,
I can only see its eyes,
They're red and sparkling like devils
And all they do is shine.

The creature reached into its cloak
And brought out a bloodstained knife,
I screamed as the creature pierced my arm,
Oh, why does it have to be at this time?

I woke up with another scream
And thought I imagined it in my head,
But no! There was blood dripping off my arm
And the dagger was still on my bed . . .

Amrita Rubens (8)
Coteford Junior School

HORSES

Horses galloping far away
Swishing their tails as they play
The grass is green, the sun can be seen
But the horses bow to me as if I am their queen
The birds can fly high in the sky
They wave to me as if to say *bye*
They fly high, high in the sky.

Charley Constable (9)
Coteford Junior School

HIM AND US

Me and my mates were so fed up
With the teacher giving us homework top-ups,
We totally despised it,
We really couldn't bear it,
We had to do something . . .
    A teacher trap!

When the kids went home,
The teacher would groan,
I hate it when children are bad,
It really drives me mad,
I have to do something . . .
    A child trap!

Helen Jones (10)
Coteford Junior School

BRIGHT LITTLE STARS

Bright stars
Yellow and gold
With little
Smiles on
Their faces

Fly left and right
Up and down
Twinkling in the sky

Shooting stars
Sprinkling white
Running fast
Right up in the sky.

Danielle Blake (8)
Coteford Junior School

WRITING A POEM

I can't write poems
I never could
And I never will
Thinking!
Thinking!
Thinking!
That's all you need to do
Says my teacher
But she doesn't know how hard it is for me
To write a poem
So I'm stuck here
Waiting!
Waiting!
Waiting!
For the literacy hour to end.

Aadam Mohammed (10)
Coteford Junior School

CATS

As black as a panther prowling the skies,
Slinky movements like a burglar at night,
Glowing lustrous emerald-green eyes,
Black silky fur swaying from side to side,
A long black tail dancing around in a whirl,
Teeth like daggers
And a big friendly smirk,
Have you guessed it yet?
A cat . . . curled up in a tiny ball . . .
Lazily lying by the flickering fire.

Priya Raju (10)
Coteford Junior School

THE BIG SHADOW

I was lying in my bed,
It was dark and very quiet,
There were shadows on the walls,
From the light in the passage.
I closed my eyes and tried to sleep,
I was drifting off, when I was woken by a real loud creak.
I jumped up and hurried to the door near my bed
And opened it to see if there was anything there.
Coming up the stairs was a real big shadow,
My stomach turned, it looked like a giant.
I ran in my room and hid under the covers,
I heard my door open, it was getting closer,
Up went my cover and I jumped out my skin,
'Night, night,' said my mum,
'And sweet dreams!'

Darren Smith (7)
Coteford Junior School

SNOW

Snow falling down on my face
As cold as a dog's nose touching my hand
Snow drifting towards the east
Everyone making snowmen in their gardens
Everything white, whiter than a cloud
Snowball fights with brothers and sisters
As someone throws the last snowball
The snowmen start to melt as the sun appears in the sky
My friends and I will never forget this day.

Rebecca Yates-Dutton (7)
Coteford Junior School

FRIENDS

Friends are good,
Friends are great.
In times of trouble they're always there,
Whether I'm sad or lonely,
They're always there to lend a hand.

They make me laugh,
They make me smile,
They make me wet my underwear,
We stick together, like good friends should,
Stronger and stronger as days pass by.

As day turns to night,
Hello turns to goodbye,
I know I'll see my friend again,
Friends are good,
But my friend is great.

Aidan Lawlor (9)
Coteford Junior School

SNOWMAN

I made a snowman when it snowed
In my garden beside the quiet road
Snow, snow here, there, everywhere
Now that's a sight very rare

I made a snowman in the cold
For the head a big ball, I rolled
Snowflakes soft as cotton wool
I hold them like a precious jewel

I made a snowman very tall
I thought to myself, *will it fall?*
Very excited I looked out, the next day
I saw my snowman had melted away . . .

Shaleena Singh (9)
Coteford Junior School

SNOW

Snow crunching under feet,
Slippery surface slipping you about.
Snowflakes fall in the neck of your coat.

Snowballs have been thrown giving a chill,
Skidding cars, going slowly.
Snowmen have been made, arms need to be finished.

Snow angel stories being made by people in the snow,
Steamy windows being wiped so the people can see.
Strong ice on car windows, drivers scraping it.

Some neighbours' cars stuck on driveways, sweeping snow away,
Stuck traffic trying a new shortcut.
Stuck in snow, call AA, they say, 'No way, not in this weather!'

Snow on the cars, they look like cubes of ice,
Some people walk through the snow, looking like snowmen.
Snow is deep, getting deeper to the knees.

School trips have been cancelled, what a shame!
School children play in the playground,
School has ended and it is time to go home.

Snow melting off the trees,
Snow disappearing from the rooftops.
Snow, oh snow, beautiful snow, why do you have to go?

Anthoney McIntosh (9)
Coteford Junior School

SNOW

Fluttering down from a gloomy sky,
Settling like a carpet,
Falling gently onto my face,
I'm happy to see the snow.

Fluttering down from a gloomy sky,
White, clean and bright,
It covers the land,
I'm happy to see the snow.

Fluttering down from a gloomy sky,
Children having fun,
Snowmen and snowballs everywhere,
I'm happy to see the snow.

Fluttering down from a gloomy sky,
Freezing cold on my cheeks,
Fingers getting numb,
I'm happy to see the snow.

Luke Rondel (7)
Coteford Junior School

PLAYING IN THE SNOW

Crisp and bright, but cold and wet.
I wrap up warm, so I can play
In my garden, which is covered with white snow today.
I build a snowman, with some help
And now I watch him melt and melt.

Oliver Cipres (7)
Coteford Junior School

MY BIRD

African parrot,
Sitting on his silver perch,
Making a racket.

Ash is his cool name
And his home is a white cage,
With bells to play with.

He scrapes his grey beak,
On his green and wooden perch,
So he keeps it clean.

On his bright white cage,
He exercises his wings,
So he learns to fly.

When it comes to night
And he falls off his bright perch,
Then he falls to sleep.

Curtis Stephan (7)
Coteford Junior School

QUIET POEMS

It was so quiet
That I heard a grasshopper sleep
It was so quiet
That I heard a fly hover a mile away
It was so quiet
That I heard a snake slither.

Chloe Morgan (8)
Coteford Junior School

THE KILLING CACTUS

Holy and silent
Banana-shaped
With a lovely pattern of furry spikes

Jagged and dry
Prickly spiked
Rigid and non-bendy lives the cactus
That stays completely put

Still and quiet
Pointed, long
Tall with a flash of dark green
But . . .
This cactus is fatal, deadly, vile and vicious.

Matthew Thomas (8)
Coteford Junior School

NAIL VARNISH

I like nail varnish,
I like them bright,
I like them when they glow in the night.

Shining, glowing, smooth as ice,
I blow on them,
So they're nice and dry.

Some smell like bubblegum,
Some smell like strawberry,
Oh, I wish I could eat them all.

Oh no! It's nail varnish,
Oh, what a shame,
I just wish that they could all be mine.

Malina Patel (8)
Coteford Junior School

SNOWMAN

Snowman, snowman melting fast
In the midday sunshine blast
You have fulfilled your winter task
Hiding behind your snowy mask
You have seen all children laugh and play
All the way through night and day

Snowman, snowman, melting fast
In the midday sunshine blast
I'm sad to say it's time to go
But, you won't be forgotten though
You have fulfilled young Katie's dream
To build you taller than she's ever seen

Snowman, snowman, melting fast
In the midday sunshine blast
You turning to a winter tear
Melting fast in the sunshine's lair
You're a prisoner to the sunshine's glow
Becoming a puddle, it's time to go

Snowman, snowman, melting fast
In the midday sunshine blast.

Elli Robertson-Walker (10)
Coteford Junior School

SNOW, SNOW

The soft snow is falling
Children with freezing fingers
Freezing to the bone
Children covered in snow
Cars sliding on the road.

Sarah Dalglish (7)
Coteford Junior School

CAKE

I crept down
Teddy in my hand
Through the open door
I see it there
The strawberry cake

I sneak in
All is quiet
But then, I hear a sound
Oh no! It's Mum
She's on the stairs

Crash, bang!
Oh no! She's heard me
Hide quickly
But don't forget the cake
Grab it and under the table

Phew!
Out of sight.

Chloe Wellington (10)
Coteford Junior School

FAIRY FRIENDS

Fairies are kind and gentle,
They float high up in the air.
Some people don't believe in them,
Some people don't even care.

I believe in fairies,
They grant your wishes and dreams.
When I'm sad they come and help me,
Until I smile and play again.

In the day when I'm happy,
I pretend I'm a fairy and fly.
I flutter my golden wings
And reach up very high.

Caroline Emma Henderson (7)
Coteford Junior School

FALCO

Falco is cool,
because he pulls.
He's the best,
he beats the rest.

He can fly high
amongst the stars.
Then he lands on a planet
called Mars.

He goes on adventures,
near the boss.
Although he's tough,
he's near a moth.

He's just like a fox
and the rest.
But they have something
like a box!

Falco is cool,
because he swims in a pool.
He's the best,
he beats the *rest!*

Christopher Thomas (10)
Coteford Junior School

SLIPPERY SLOPES

We're going abroad to learn to ski
Upon the slopes of Italy
My dad went skiing years ago
And soon was whizzing on the snow
Then one day he went too fast
The rocks and trees went flying past
He didn't see the precipice
Until it was too late to miss
He went flying through the air
As though he didn't have a care
Until he landed in a tree
And hung there for the world to see
They rescued him at half-past three
And gave him cakes and cups of tea
They told him some important things:-
Don't go flying without your wings
And don't race towards a precipice
Unless you know just where it is.

Cara Morbey (11)
Coteford Junior School

THE WEATHER

The sky grew darker and darker,
Then came the thunderstorm and the lightning struck,
Immediately the heaviest rain ever came down.
It poured and poured,
Almost as soon as it started, it stopped,
The sky was clear and bright,
The rainbow appeared in its beautiful colours,
To fulfil the promise.

Tolulope Obileye (7)
Coteford Junior School

EVERY TIME

Every time I see you,
You make me smile.
Every time you leave me,
You make me feel sad.
Every time you're near me,
You make me feel secure.
Every time you talk to me,
You make my troubles drift away
Every time we go somewhere,
We always have such fun.
Every time I tell you something,
I know I can trust you.
Every time I'm feeling lonely,
You always cheer me up.
Every time I'm around you,
You make me happy.
Every time you're with me,
I know I have a friend.

Sarah Bennett (11)
Coteford Junior School

GREECE

I wish I was in Greece with my family,
In the sun next to the deep blue sea,
Wearing my goggles, going into the water,
With the waves going over me.
As I am swimming in the sea,
Lots of fish are around me,
The fish are so colourful and beautiful,
Swimming in the deep blue sea.

Carissa Odle (8)
Coteford Junior School

AMAZONIA

The flowing sapphire-blue river meanders through the tranquil
rainforest.
The emerald-green leaves rustle as a gigantic hawk takes flight from a
huge tree.
The dripping ruby-red blood from the leftovers of the monstrous
crocodile's meal sinks into the soft, muddy soil.
The opal-white flowers provide the atmosphere with a sweet-smelling
aroma to add to its fantastic appearance.
The multicoloured rainbow stretches longer than the river as the rain
and sun draw in the battle of weather.
Welcome to Amazonia.

Aaron Raju (10)
Coteford Junior School

SADNESS

Lying in the corner, all alone,
A blanket of blackness covering my soul,
Body cold,
Beads of sweat running down my face,
Darkness filling the room,
Nothing else matters,
Why, oh why did this happen?

Sadness winding through the room like a snake,
Lying,
Thinking,
Pain sinking in like a dagger into a body,
When it dawned into my soul,
A shiver ran down my spine,
Why, oh why did it happen . . . to me?

Kate Kidd-Rossiter (10)
Coteford Junior School

GOLF

Ping of the club,
the swish of the ball,
as it goes through the air.

You must hope it goes over there,
in the hole or you're in despair.

But when push comes to shove,
you have to remember,
to buy a new . . .
club!

(Or maybe . . . I suppose it could be that . . .
I need to practice some more!)

Ben Barnby (11)
Coteford Junior School

MY BROTHER!

My brother is a monster
And he drives me mad
He messes up my room
And says he never has

My brother is a monster
And he drives me mad
He uses all my stuff
And says he never has

My brother is a monster
And he drives me mad
But I love my little brother
He's the best one I could have.

Joe Spires (10)
Coteford Junior School

SEASONS!

Spring
All the winter blues have gone, now all the birds are singing a song,
Leaves sprout out of the trees,
As the spring breeze rustles through my hair,
Easter eggs are fun to eat, *mmm*, what a treat,
Animals begin to creep out of hibernation,
As babies take their first glimpses of the world.

Summer!
The summer sun has just begun,
Rising in the sky above the clouds, oh so high,
Laughter fills the air, sweat covers our body,
Bumblebees scattered across the sky, *buzz, buzz,*
We sit in the shade, drinking lemonade,
As rays of light beam on our body.

Autumn!
Leaves begin to fall from the gnarled trees,
Children dress up in scary outfits, *rooarrr,*
Bright lights decorate the skies and eyes beam in excitement,
The paths have a mixture of mud and leaves,
As we mix them together with our muddy wellies.

Winter!
A white layer of snow covers the earth,
We put on our gloves and scarves with our hat with a bobble on top,
We stop and pick up a snowball . . .
We let out a scream and our mums tell us off for being mean,
We wake up at Christmas early, our bodies full of excitement,
We open our presents in a hurry, starting with the biggest,
Start to play and it lasts all day.

Sarah Goodchild (11)
Coteford Junior School

SCHOOL

School is very boring,
Most of us are snoring.
The teacher wakes us up,
By smashing a delicate cup.
Then we go for a run
And our teacher eats a buttery bun.
The big bell rings,
While the whole school sings.
Then we all go into the school,
Which is not very cool.
In the big brown hall,
Staff set up a stall.
Then it starts snowing
And the wind starts blowing.
The ground looks wet,
So does our little pet.
Then we get back to our work
And our teacher goes berserk.
Then we go in for our lunch
And we hear *munch, munch, munch.*
The girls play with skipping ropes
And we all run down steep slopes.
The teacher calls us in
And we all hide in a wheelie bin.
The teacher shouts and screams,
While we all eat ice creams.
The teacher starts burping,
While we all start slurping.
We all go home
And our teacher turns into a gnome.

Kabir Kharbanda (8)
Coteford Junior School

SOMEONE SPECIAL

Someone to love
Someone to hold
Someone to treasure
Until you grow old
When you're scared
Or feeling bad
There to make you smile
There to make you glad
Someone to take you places you've never been
Sights you only see in your wildest dreams
Places only garden fairies have seen
Someone to tell you right from wrong
Someone to share a romantic song
That someone can be anyone
But to me that's my mum.

Charlotte Gailey (11)
Coteford Junior School

THE SUN

A great globe of fire and light,
The king of the skies;
A light to the paths of the Earth.
Storms abroad seek to be his foe
And the pale moon his faithful, forever friend.

His travel across the blue of the sky,
Is what brings us day and night.
He never fails a journey across
And always makes it towards the west.

Amy Ward (11)
Coteford Junior School

WINTER'S WIND

When winter's wind
Touches ponds and trees
In gives them a sparkly gleam

Freezing everything that passes
And giving its touch of death
To all plants

Some people lighting fires and others
Drawing such a scene

No sound
Just whistling
No cars on the road
Just cold air and ice
Winter's breath is all I hear.

Jasmeet Matharu (10)
Coteford Junior School

SNOW

Snow has fallen everywhere,
Glistening and glimmering.
In the dawning, misty sunlight,
Icy ponds shimmer, icicles twinkle.
Snow is dancing, twirling round,
Like delicate snow-white feathers.
I kick the cold, cottony carpet
Up into the frosty winter breeze
And it showers silently down.
I catch arctic candyfloss
On the tip of my warm, moist tongue
And it dissolves instantly away.

Sarah Gratton (8)
Coteford Junior School

THE MOON

A face smiling in the darkness,
Never to be disturbed
From its endless chase for night.

Silently lighting the Earth
With its gentle glow,
Enticing the world into a deep slumber.

A single eye keeping watch,
Until the sun returns,
God's torch under the blanket of night.

Ross Allen (10)
Coteford Junior School

WATERFALL

Waterfall, waterfall,
Wonderful waterfall,
You're so fast,
As you run past.

Waterfall, waterfall,
Beautiful waterfall,
As you run down your slippery spine,
Onto a straight line.

Waterfall, waterfall,
Magnificent waterfall,
You're as colourful as a rainbow,
As the sun shines upon you.

Shelbie Franks (9)
Coteford Junior School

ATOMIC FIREBALL

I pick up the red-headed missile
And pull out a red ball
Roll it between my fingers and thumbs
And
Pop

Into my mouth it goes
I lick my lips
My mouth goes warm
Hot, boiling, ouch!
I spit it in the loo and it looks like a ball of blood
And I see it was a cinnamon-flavoured atomic fireball!

Daniel Parry (9)
Coteford Junior School

THE SEA

The whisper of the palm trees,
Swaying in the wind.
Gold shining sand surrounds my feet.
The lapping of the waves onto my toes.
Small pebbles getting swept in and out.
The blazing sun sparkles on the sea.
Boats sailing on the horizon.
The dolphins leap through the air,
Their skins look silky in the sun.
Tropical fish swim around my feet.
Just me and the beautiful, calm sea!

Alex Davis (11)
Coteford Junior School

My Mum

She makes me laugh
She doesn't make me cry
She's the one I ask questions
When I want to know why
She keeps me safe
She keeps me sound
She's always there
When I want her around
She makes me feel better
When I'm feeling ill
She's good with the cooker
The oven and the grill
She tells me off
If I am bad
But she's my mum
And of that I am glad.

Zoe Edwards (10)
Coteford Junior School

Summer Fun

Summer's just begun,
Time for happiness and fun,
Now they'll be eating lollies,
Instead of playing dollies!
Finally it's hot,
Unlike winter when it's not,
So out comes the golden sun,
Now it's holiday, lots of fun!

Rebecca Dalglish (10)
Coteford Junior School

A SNOWY DAY

The snow glistens like diamonds
Trees frozen in blocks of ice
Snowflakes sparkle like emeralds
Fluttering down like angels
The snow is soft as powder trickling through your fingers
Everywhere are icy roads, cars slipping and sliding along
Children tobogganing down steep hills
Laughing and screaming
The children make snowmen using coal as buttons and eyes
They use carrots for noses
Everyone loves a snowball fight.

Luke O'Brien (8)
Coteford Junior School

THE SINGER

The singer arrives on the floor
Tapping the microphone to a roar.

The crowd applaud, clap, clap, clap
He clears his voice, chat, chat, chat

The pianist tickles in preparation
The brass section hoot in participation

The house lights fade like the setting sun
And the spotlight shines on his happy mum

He bursts into song with a familiar tune
Delighting the crowd very soon.

James Ketteridge (11)
Coteford Junior School

SNOW

It drifts, swaying swiftly from side to side, like silver pearls flowing
from the cotton clouds.
Then gently and silently it touches the ground, cuddling into a white
mountain, without a sound to be heard but the whisper of the wind.
Footprints disappear within a murmur of a bird tapping onto a
gleaming white tree.

The world turns into a winter fantasy and people turn into
live snowmen.
It whirls around in the sky and brushes hands as it gently falls and
makes people tingle.
Its smooth and silky feel makes everything come to life.
Rocky hills turn into soft cushions, houses turn to mountains of snow
and tree branches turn into skeleton fingers.
As the snow dances in the air and children play and their faces brighten
the sky turns black, as black as ink, as black as the darkest blanket.
Eventually children get sleepy and their eyes begin to gently close, they
put their heads to the soft pillow dreaming of the day that awaited them.

Tamar Ayres (10)
Coteford Junior School

ANIMALS

A nteaters search for ants because they're very hungry of course
N ice, cold ice is where polar bears live
I n the tallest of the trees are bright coloured parrots
M onkeys swing from tree to tree sometimes scratching their armpits
A ntelopes run as fast as they can before the lions catch them
L eopards are quietly getting ready to catch their prey
S limy snakes slither through the jungle aiming where to
                                      shoot his venom

If you go to a paradise like this I'm sure you'll say it's enchanted.

Hannah Victoria Monk (8)
Coteford Junior School

GLISTENING, GLOWING SNOW

When you see the night sky,
With the snowflakes falling,
You wonder why it's snowing,
The icicles hang from roof to roof,
The pure white blanket of snow,
Which looks like frosty sequences,
Glisten and glow,
You see it snow and snow and the next it's melted,
Outside, people make snowmen and big snowballs,
It makes you joyful and just makes you calm,
You go outside to play in the drifting snow,
The trees have gone from green to frosty white,
Then you look out of the window and see children on sledges,
It snows in winter and I wish it never ended,
When it melts, a sign of happiness and love drifts off.

Simren Degun (8)
Coteford Junior School

GOD

You, they all say are our Lord
Be it here or abroad
Creator of the sun and the rain
Maker of peace and the of pain
The people were just the title
Truth and love came after the Bible
Her and I, I believe
Came after Adam and Eve
When I think of you, God
All the pain and grief I relieve.

Yanil Patel (7)
Coteford Junior School

BABIES

What I hate about babies
Is when they cry and scream

What I like about babies
Is when they are cute and cuddly

What I hate about babies
Is that they don't listen and knock things off the table

What I like about babies
Is when you tickle them and they laugh in the cutest way ever

What I hate about babies
Is when they spit food out when they are eating

What I like about babies
Is when they waddle around like ducks

What I hate about babies
Is that they disturb you when you're watching a film

What I like about babies
Is when they try to dance to music on the radio

What I hate about babies
Is that they break my toys

What I like about babies
Is that they can give you a cheeky smile

What I hate about babies
Is that they dribble over you when you hold them

What I like about babies
Is when they give you a nice cuddle

What I hate about babies
Is that they sometimes pinch you

What I like about babies
Is when they cuddle their toys in bed

What I hate about babies
Is they cry when they don't get their own way

What I like about babies
Is when they amazingly fall asleep in your arms.

Daniel Harrington (7)
Coteford Junior School

IF . . .

If I was a bird,
Oh joy to me,
I would sweep and soar,
Over the sea,
Over hills and trees
By busy bees.

If I was a deer,
Oh joy to me,
I would prance and dance,
Over the grass,
Fleeing at a hunter's gun,
Or playing - having fun.

If I was fish,
Oh joy to me,
Diving deep in the sea,
Or swimming along happily,

Or hiding from the . . .

Shark!

Alexandra Shaw (11)
Coteford Junior School

SCHOOL

I've just woken up on a sunny bright day
I can't wait to go to school
It's my friend's birthday
The school day has just begun
It's 8.45 and the bell has just rung!
We start by sitting ourselves down
And the teacher takes the register
Just in case of a fire
We have maths then English
ICT and topic
But then I drift away . . .
'Zoe, pay attention, you should be listening!'
The end of the day is just about to come
I've had a good day
But I can't wait to see my mum!

Zoe Huggett (9)
Coteford Junior School

STAR

Star in the nightly sky
The sky would not be so beautiful
Without you

Star in the nightly sky
You twinkle like silver diamonds

Star in the nightly sky
You look like sparks of fireworks
That just went bang

Star in the daytime sky
I am sad, where are you?

Isabel Foley (8)
Coteford Junior School

ATTACK OF THE TOOTHBRUSH

In my morning I wake up,
I hear the birds talking to each other,
They are sheltering on branches of trees,
My eyes aren't used to the light,
So I squint a little,
I walk out of my bedroom,
Still squinting,
I meet my dad who tells me to brush my teeth,
I head towards the bathroom,
In search of the deadly monster (my toothbrush),
I find the swamp 'goo' (my toothpaste),
Lift them towards each other,
Then towards me,
My teeth attack first,
It spreads all around my mouth,
It was over in a 'spit' second,
'Victory'
'I defeated the deadly monster,
Long live me,'
But . . . a problem, it's going to be back tomorrow.

Sophie Harris-Edmond (8)
Coteford Junior School

OSTRICH

Ostriches are big
Ostriches are fat
Ostriches can be better than that
Ostriches can run fast
And lay large eggs
They keep them warm
Between their long pink legs.

Lauren Currivan (7)
Coteford Junior School

PANTZ

Ya gotta love 'em 'cause
Ya gotta wear 'em

There're . . .

Stripy ones
Spotty ones
Red ones
Black ones
Polka dot too

You pull them down when you go to the loo

There're . . .

Frilly ones
Woolly ones
Green ones
Purple ones
Mixed with blue

You pull them down when you go to the loo

There're . . .

Cotton ones
Warm ones
Yellow ones
England ones too

You pull them down when you go to the loo

There're . . .

Towelling ones
Hot pantz
Shaded ones
Animal ones
Some thongs too

You pull them up when you've finished with the loo!

Christopher Arnold (11)
Coteford Junior School

IN MY MAGIC FLYING SHIP

In my magic flying ship
with multicoloured sails
I fly away to the North Pole
I watch the baby seals
and their mothers too

In my magic flying ship
with multicoloured sails
I fly away to the Caribbean
over the children picking up fruit
bananas, pineapples and mangoes too

In my magic flying ship
with multicoloured sails
I fly away to Australia
I look down on the sandy beaches
watching children splashing in the sea

In my magic flying ship
with multicoloured sails
I am now tucked up in bed
with all the dreams
still dancing in my head.

Ruth Sarah Barclay (8)
Coteford Junior School

TIMOTHY'S BUG

Timothy, Timothy, Timothy's bug,
Timothy's locked in Wormwood Scrubs.
'But why?' I hear you call aloud,
So I'll tell you a tale of why guilty he was found.

It was a cold and misty morn,
When Timothy tripped up on a thorn
And there beneath him he felt a squirm,
He pulled it out, a pinstripe worm!

He took it home, it was five foot long,
It kept on making bangs and bongs.
So he sold it to an old gravedigger,
Who asked for a refund 'cause it just grew bigger.

He gave it to his cousin's mother,
But she gave it back 'cause it bit her brother.
He lent it to the Barclays Bank,
Where it ate the money and grew to the size of an army tank.

The brickwork crumbled, the foundations burst;
As the immense pink monster devoured a church.
'Whose worm is this?' said an officer with a bellow,
Tim crept forward, a sickly yellow.

'Why couldn't you leave nature be?
That worm's bigger than a redwood tree.'
Then the worm transformed into a butterfly
And it sailed away to the distant sky.

Now, of course, the end of my tale,
Timothy was locked up in jail!

Charlotte James (10)
Coteford Junior School

Your Fault!

Have you ever had an argument about where to eat with your
brother or sister?
Yes, I thought so.
This is how mine goes . . .

'Where do you want to go for lunch?' Dad says.
'McDonald's!' Joe says.
'No! KFC,' I say.
'Wimpy?' Jack says.
'I know, Pizza Hut,' Joe says.
'Chicken wings . . . yuk! Pizza Express,' I say.
'Wimpy!' Jack says.
'Got it! Burger King,' Joe says.
'The chips are greasy! Fish and chips,' I say.
'*Wimpy*!' Jack says.
'Right, you three, where does Jack want to go?' Dad says.
'Wimpy,' Jack says.
'Wimpy it is,' Dad says.
'Oh, I hate Wimpy!' I say.
'McDonald's!' Joe says.
'No, KFC!' I say
And so it goes on . . .
'Til he doesn't take us anywhere.

'Why did Joe have to start it over again?'
'I didn't start it again!' Joe says.
'Yes you did,' I say.
'No I didn't!'
'Yes you did!'
And so it goes on . . .
'Til we get sent to our rooms.

'This is all your fault Joe,' I say.

Helen Scibilia (11)
Coteford Junior School

THOUSANDS OF MIRRORS

Hundreds and thousands of mini mirrors surround us,
Shining, sparkling, shimmering, reflecting from the beautiful
Light from the crystal chandeliers.
Dancing beams like glimmering diamonds.
Wonderful silver shapes tell their own story.
Surrounded by gold, green and blue jewels,
It is not my imagination,
It's a mausoleum of the family of the prophet (peace be upon him).

A golden dome, walls of painted tiles, blue, white, green and red,
Tall thin towers with loud speakers calling the people for their prayers.

Muhaddisa Datoo (9)
Coteford Junior School

FAMILY HOLIDAYS

F amily holidays are fun!
A ll the water parks to see
M aybe Dad will swim with me
I   ce creams pink, blue and green
L ovliest, scrummiest I've ever seen
Y ippee, yippee, I love the sea!

H appy children playing about
O ver here they all shout
'L ook everybody, I've found a fish'
I   want to keep it, I wish, I wish
D ig and dig to get some treasure
A picnic they found was quite a pleasure
Y ipee, yippee, I love the sea!

That was the best day there will ever be.

Rebecca Hanington (9)
Coteford Junior School

Sweet Toffee

Long-sleeper
Snow-eater
Fast-sprinter
Naughty-jumper

Big-leaper
Bread-snatcher
Feet-warmer
Cushion-stealer

Plate-licker
Toy-taker
Bone-chewer
Garden-lover.

Matthew Gleeson (9)
Coteford Junior School

Cat

Silent-sneaker
Leg-rubber
Heat-lover
Skin-scraper
Food-eater
Mouse-catcher
Quiet-pouncer
Milk-drinker
People-annoyer
Plump-sleeper
What am I?
I'm a cat!

Rhys Bradbury (9)
Coteford Junior School

MY PET

Soft, small
Fluffy
Quick and speedy
Hyperactive
Hairy, bushy
Jumpy, nervous
Chews and nibbles
Squeaky, sneaky
Beady eyes
Sniffy nose
Sharp teeth
Blunt little tail
Four paws
Sticking-up ears
Short whiskers
Skittering
Scratchy
Lightweight
Squeezy and squashy
Through pipes and holes
Climbs and hangs
Nocturnal
Tucked away, hidden
Golden brown
Vegetarian
Seed eater
Lots of fun
The best pet in the world
Who am I?

Elliott Coghill (9)
Coteford Junior School

CAT

I see a cat
asleep in the sun
its chest rising and falling
as it breathes
its fur black as night

Coiled up like a spring
sleek and soft as a
feather bed
proud as a queen
with emerald eyes
silently snoozing
without a care in the world

A mouse meanders by
unaware of a malevolent eye
opening . . .

The mouse turns

Miaow!

It bolts
cat in hot pursuit
round and round they go
any second now . . .

Snap!

Kristina Greally (9)
Coteford Junior School

A GOLDEN BEACH

A golden beach
Golden sand under your feet
You sit on it
Run on it
Play on it
Sometimes you even lay on it
A golden beach

A golden beach
Sparkling and bright
Beneath the sun, it looks so nice
Children play on it from morning till night

A golden beach
You sit on the sand
And watch the sea, the roaring waves get closer to me.

Jade Short (9)
Coteford Junior School

BATS, BATS, BATS!

At dusk, at night
Squeaking, squeaking
Navigating, hunting
Silently flying

Skinny, silky wings
Bony, triangular wings
Furry, silky body
Small, oval body
Miniature head, circular face
Small mouth, moist nose
Pond bat!

Helen Townsend (8)
Coteford Junior School

HOLIDAYS

I've had many holidays
Each one rather fun
As well as sea, sand and palm trees
I can't wait to see the sun

I nearly always dream of flying away in a plane
On my way to Australia
And then back again

I just love playing on the beach
With sand between my toes
But after being in the sea
I get a very cold nose

I've had many holidays
Soon I'll have another one
So why don't you come along
We could have lots of fun!

Rebecca Smith (8)
Coteford Junior School

THE WEATHER

Winter is here,
It's that time of year,
The cold wind is biting,
Perhaps I'll go kiting.

The sky has turned grey,
It's snowing today,
It's coming down fast,
I hope that it lasts.

Joe Griffiths (9)
Coteford Junior School

MY AUNTY HAS A BABY

My aunty has a baby
He has really grown
And sometimes when he's angry
He moans and moans and moans

My aunty has a baby
He is full of fun
But he gets very smelly
When we need to change his bum

My aunty has a baby
I think he's really cute
But I really don't like it
When he covers me in puke

My aunty has a baby
I love him, yes I do
He's really, really lovely
And I think he loves me too.

Jade Spires (9)
Coteford Junior School

THE SUN

The sun is the brightest sight
The sun makes me full of delight
Even though it never comes out at night

The sun is round and full of rays
It can brighten the dullest of days
Making me want to celebrate and praise.

Kathryn Sansby (9)
Coteford Junior School

SNOW

I have never woken up to snow
Then one day it was there
Like a white blanket lying over the street
Cars were hidden under the powdery, soft snow
I was so excited, I rubbed my eyes, was I dreaming?

I rushed to school wrapped up in layers of clothes
The snow was so cold it was like being trapped inside a freezer
I didn't have any gloves but the excitement warmed me up

A teacher ruined our fun, making us go into school
But the fun had only just begun
Teachers can't watch children all the time
Sneaking snow into my pockets, droplets of water fell to the floor
School had ended, hooray, time to play

I woke up this morning, excited again
But to my horror, the snow had gone.

Max Pendry (11)
Coteford Junior School

WHAT IS IT?

It splashes
It falls
It's continuous
It's colossal
It's icy
It's foamy
It's attractive and beautiful
What is it?
Niagara Falls.

Bhadrika Parmar (8)
Coteford Junior School

THE END

To see the end of the world come today,
What a sight it would be for me,
While others run and scream and cry,
I would sit and think of life gone by.

I would think of days when I had fun,
I would think of days when I wanted to run,
I would think of days when I felt alone,
I would think of days when I would cry down the phone,
To the people dying all around
And try and wonder how they were found

And sometimes I wish I had never been born,
But since I married my life on this earth,
I have sworn my duties to her,
To fight for more peace and fresh air,
For mine and many children's lungs.

Leah Davies (10)
Coteford Junior School

SPRINGTIME

S   pringtime brings children,
P   eople walking about like lost sheep,
R   ain might come and grow your crops,
I   deal weather for barbeques,
N   ice flowers to pick,
G   reen lush grass flows with the wind,
T   ime doesn't matter, you can stay up late,
I   see lots of lovely days to come,
M   en and women relax in the sun,
E   verybody enjoys spring!

Sanam Batavia (8)
Coteford Junior School

WHY?

Why are the trees green, Dad?
Why did my dog eat the cat?
Why is Mum taller than you, Dad?
Why are you growing fat?

Why are some people stupid, Dad?
Why are some people smart?
Why do I wake up at 7am, Dad?
Why am I not good at art?

Why do you think I am noisy, Dad?
Why do you think I am bad?
Why aren't you listening to me, Dad?
Why am I boring you, Dad?

Arik Rubens (9)
Coteford Junior School

AUTUMN LEAVES

Crunching leaves
Golden
Brown
Crunching under your feet
Crunch
Crunch
Crunch
Leaves drifting down from trees
Having a lovely flight
Down
Down
Down
Like a floating piece of paper.

Dominique Lawrence (10)
Coteford Junior School

THE RACE

The cheering starts,
The lights turn on,
All the racers accelerate.

Right, here we go!
Round the corner,
Oops, steady now, don't want to crash.

The tension's on;
Hands start to sweat,
I've abolished them all, but wait . . .

Who's that ahead?
I use a boost;
To fly ahead like an eagle.

He knocks me down;
I lose control,
I crash into the solid wall!

'Argh!' I holler,
As I jump up;
But wait a second, where am I?

I'm not on track;
I'm in my bed,
Oh why! Oh why! I moan; oh why!

Kavil Patel (11)
Coteford Junior School

BORED

Clock on the wall ticking like nobody's business,
There's me, flicking time away,
Nothing to do,
Outside it rains,
What a pain!

TV's in for service,
Best friend's in Venice,
What a life eh!
There's me flicking time away!

Shiv Kharbanda (11)
Coteford Junior School

BANANAS

Bananas, bananas,
Bananas are the best,
Nice, smooth middle
In a bright-yellow vest,
Green ones,
Yellow ones,
Everywhere you go,
Bananas, bananas,
High and low,
You take them from
A nice high tree,
You take them from
A nice low bowl,
You peel the skin
Off the bananas,
Put them in the
Bowl of cream,
Bananas, bananas,
Everyone loves them,
Bananas, bananas,
Everyone eats them,
But I don't!

Ashleigh Coombs (10)
Coteford Junior School

SPROUTS

I hate sprouts,
They're icky sprouts,
I hate sprouts,
They make me feel sick, sprouts.

I have to have them on Christmas Day,
I try not to be sick when I go out and play,
Can't help it though they're 'orrible.

We always argue on Christmas Day,
'You can 'ave the last sprout!'
'No, you can!' I shout.

It just sits there . . .
Staring back at me.
'What do you want?' I asked it,
It still just sat there.

I picked it up
And put it in a cup,
I hate sprouts,
They're horrible sprouts.

I hate sprouts,
They're icky sprouts,
I hate sprouts,
They make me feel sick, sprouts!

Frances Millman (10)
Coteford Junior School

THE DAY BEFORE CHRISTMAS

The day before Christmas
The hustle and bustle
Of last-minute shopping

The excitement of children
In anticipation of their presents
The rustle of paper
As Mother wraps the gifts

Father rushes off to get the tree
To put the gifts under

The twinkle of bright lights
The fairy perched high on the tree

The aroma from the kitchen
As Mother bakes mince pies

A knock at the door
Just friends saying, 'Merry Christmas.'

As the night draws in all around
The glow of coloured lights come on
The children tucked in
Mother and Father have a break at last

All is worthwhile to see
Their faces on Christmas Day.

Becky Robinson (9)
Coteford Junior School

A HERO

A figure bold and strong,
Who will never let himself go wrong,
Always leads himself in the right direction
And always makes his moves with perfection.
Defeating bad guys everywhere,
Under the sea,
At the lair,
Above the sky,
Risking his spiky, gelled hair.

Louis Monckton (10)
Coteford Junior School

THE SEA

The sea is so gentle,
It sways making a song of sweetness to my ears,
It is so peaceful; I love it like a heart,
I listen to the sea all the time, its beautiful song sings to me.

Matthew Harris (8)
Coteford Junior School

SNOW!

Snow is like a white quilt covering the town,
Take your sledges up the hill and slide down.
Freezing fingers and tingling toes, into the warm where the fire glows.
Sparkling like sequins where the sunlight shines,
Then melting away leaving grey slush behind.

Fleur Harman (9)
Coteford Junior School

WIND DOGS

Here come the wind dogs,
Lapping at my face.
Ruffling up my hair,
Not now wind dogs, it's not time to play!

Here come the wind dogs,
Running around my legs,
Now they're getting excited,
Watch out! Not today!

Here come the wind dogs,
Tugging at my coat,
Ripping at my hands,
Time to shoo them away!

Where are the wind dogs?
Normally nipping at my nose,
Why don't they play with me today?
Oh well, maybe another day!

Jessica Henderson (10)
Coteford Junior School

SOUTH AFRICA

Cape Town where the weather is fine
Is famous for its wine
We went up the mountain in a cable car
To have a great view of the city
We also went to Cape Point to see the two oceans meet
We saw the penguins on the beach
But sadly
They were out of reach!

Chris Hills (10)
Coteford Junior School

A CAT'S LIFE!

My cat is a creature,
With four legs and a tail,
He likes to go out and sit on a rail,
Also he sits by the fire, all cosy and warm
And at night-time he likes to go out for a walk.
He goes under the hedges to look for some mice,
But never finds one, all day and all night,
He miaows at the window so he can come in,
To look for his dinner out of a tin.
Which everyone says is fit for a king,
His milk in a dish, ready to sip,
It really is funny if you look at his lips,
His tongue goes all curly,
His eyebrows go up,
He looks just like me drinking tea from a cup.
When his tummy is full,
He stretches out wide,
He looks up to tell me, I'm off to hide!
He curls his long tail and creeps up the stairs,
He doesn't believe we know that he is there.
Into the bedroom he quietly creeps,
Gets into the cupboard and falls fast asleep,
He has lots of dreams in his little catnap,
But comes back down to sit on my lap,
His purring gets louder, he snuggles right down,
All of a sudden, we don't hear a sound.
Finally he wakes and looks up to me,
Hello little cat, it's me, Charlie.
I look down at him and he looks back to me,
Have I told you his name? It's little Terry!

Charlie May (9)
Coteford Junior School

MY LITTLE BROTHER AND MY LITTLE SISTER

My little brother picks his nose
My little brother picks his toes
My little sister licks her lips
My little sister sways her hips

My little brother watches TV
My little brother jumps on me
My little sister is always talking
My little sister is slow at walking

My little brother likes to fight
My little brother cycles out of sight
My little sister does her hair
My little sister doesn't like a scare

My little brother likes playing Power Rangers
My little brother trains with Ruislip Rangers
My little sister doesn't like peas
My little sister likes red cheese

My little brother would like a pet
My little brother wants a Star Wars set
My little sister likes to cook
My little sister loves her books

In the end
I have to say
My little brother is great fun
My little sister is a happy one.

Gavin Barclay (10)
Coteford Junior School

THERE'S SOMETHING UNDER MY BED

There's something under my bed,
It's big and scary and it looks like sand.
What if it's Sandman?
There's something under my bed,
I can hear it, it sounds like the Tin Man, it's very loud.
There's something under my bed,
I'm going to have a look now.
It looks hairy, it looks like sand,
It's running towards me . . .
It's my dog, Gemma, a golden retriever.

Amy Kenny (11)
Coteford Junior School

MEAL TIME

Now, when I have a meal,
I've got my special ways,
I've always got my favourite food
And my mother always says,
'Why on earth do you eat like that
And leave the best to last?'
But I don't reply, I've heard it all before
Thousands and thousands of times,
How shall I choose all these lovely desserts?
Trifle or chocolate mud pie?
I really must stop, I think I will pop . . .
Bang!

Kerry Stack (10)
Coteford Junior School

TEETH OUT

It all started
When I went to a dentist
In London,
On the way there,
There was a train delay
And even when I got to the dentist's
I had to wait for hours,
With itchy stickers on my arms
And cream on my hands.
When it was my turn,
I sat in a bed
And they put a needle into my hand.
Ow!
Then there was this horrible feeling,
Creeping up my arm,
When it got to my head,
I felt nothing more . . .
Until I woke up crying,
My gums were really sore.
They led me from the bed to a comfy chair,
I was still crying,
'Not havin' anymore teeth out!'
Later I thought,
'Did the dentist cut a hole in my cheek
And reach in with a tool to get my teeth?'
My mouth was closed,
I'm glad it's over.

William Pearmain (9)
Coteford Junior School

MITSY, MY RESCUE DOG

Mitsy was cold
Mitsy was lonely
Mitsy was cuddly and lovely

One day a family came
They looked at Mitsy
Mitsy put her paws up on the cage
She looked sweet

She was desperate
She wanted to find a home
And in her dog language she said
'Please, please love me
Please take me home'

And when I stuck my fingers through the cage
She licked them
She kissed them
She wagged her tail like mad
She did not bark
She was not like the other noisy dogs

She made me want to cry
And I said to Mum,
'Please can we have this doggy?'
She said, 'I think she will be just right.'

Five months later, Mitsy is still lovely and cuddly
And she's lost that desperate look of
'Please take me home'
Because now she is home!

Martin James (9)
Coteford Junior School

THE NIGHT THE MUSEUM CAME TO LIFE

Skeletons too old for display,
Tales never told,
All to be locked away.

The halls are dark,
With no kind of spark,
The dinosaurs rule the hall.

The corridor's pitch-black,
Rooftops with a luminous presence,
Skeletons fill the air.

The dinos come alive,
They're doing a jive,
We're having a disco, yeah.

They stomp their feet,
Whilst dancing to the rocky beat,
As they trample the vast floor.

Suddenly the dinos froze,
As they touched their enormous toes,
The amazingly scary T-rex rose.

Then he lifted his almighty head
And bellowed out,
'It's time for bed!'

Benjamin Shaw (9)
Coteford Junior School

NOISE

Noise is like a drum banging
Noise is like fire crackling
Noise is like a glass breaking
Noise is like an earthquake erupting
Noise is like a house falling
Noise is like an animal roaring
Noise is like a bomb exploding
What is noise? Noise is loud!

Khiszer Butt (8)
Coteford Junior School

WINTER

'Winter, winter!'
It's a lovely day
Just like the snow
Falling on the streets
The snow stops falling then
It starts to rain
The rain makes the snow melt
All day
And then it stops and starts
To snow again, it snows so fast
On the streets
The streets with so much
Snow starting to get high
So we make a snowman
Then we play
'Snowball fight'!

Mariam Jussab (8)
Hambrough Primary School

WINTER

Winter is cold,
It happened a long time ago,
So it is old,
Snow falls down,
In the big town,
It's a happy day today,
Hip, hip, hooray,
We're having a lovely time,
People singing, dancing, singing a rhyme,
Throwing snowballs,
Making Christmas calls,
Snow is white,
It looks so bright,
Snow, snow, please come again,
You are as beautiful as my golden chain.

Aileen Suresh (9)
Hambrough Primary School

WINTER

Snowflakes, cornflakes
Falling from the sky
Snowflakes, cornflakes
White and small
Snowflakes, hornflakes
Kiss the snow and make it cry
Snowflakes, wornflakes
Nice and cold.

Sunil Mair (8)
Hambrough Primary School

SNOW BELLS

Dolphins, dolphins play in the cold
Dolphins, dolphins, snow is old

Snow, snow you fall
Snow you are like a round ball

Snow, snow, you are a trickle tool
Snow, snow, you are cool

Polar bear, polar bear, you are a naughty fool
Polar bear, polar bear, you are cool

Chirstam Shool
Is an April fool

Christmas Day
Is the month of play

School play
Is a day in May

If we eat Christmas food
You can think good.

Pratichi Vaghela (9)
Hambrough Primary School

SNOW!

Snow, snow falling from the sky!
Come and blow the wind,
Can you hear me cry?
Snow, snow, how powerful you seem!
Coming from *blizzards.*
You are gentle and fragile!

Hardeep Bharj (9)
Hambrough Primary School

ANIMALS

I am a snake
As troublesome as can be
I wake up a lion
He runs after me

I am a rabbit
As hoppy as can be
Hoppity hop
Jumping up and down
Enjoying other rabbits
Jumping up is my hobby

I am a cat
That likes to eat
I'm fierce and strong
I tripped next-door's dog
I am fierce

I am a lion
I like bossing others around
I boss the snake
I boss the bear
I'm a bossy, bossy lion

I am a bear
As lazy as can be
I always sleep
I'm eating
Sleeping and dreaming
I am a lazy bear
That's me

We're all different animals
With different animals.

Asha Jimale (9)
Hambrough Primary School

SNOWFLAKES

Snowflake, snowflake come to me
Snowflake, snowflake you're mine
Snowflake, snowflake come here
Snowflake, snowflake come back
Snowflake, snowflake build me
A snowman just for me
Snowflake, snowflake you're in my heart
Snowflake, snowflake you're cold like me
Nice and soft and nice to play with
Snowflake, snowflake stay with me all the time
Make the snowflake blizzard down for everybody
Snowflake, snowflake you're frosty
Snowflake, snowflake make me ice-skate
Snowflake, snowflake be windy and rainy
To make it colder and icier
Oh, some people wear jumpers
Gloves, hats and coats
But I don't because I love the cold air
It smells fresh
Snowflake, snowflake I'm here for you
Stay here forever, always come every Christmas
Winter is always coming to me in Sathall.

Gurpreet Matharou (9)
Hambrough Primary School

SNOWFLAKES

Snowflake, snowflake how do you do?
The children are all waiting to play with you
Snowflake, snowflake when will you fall?
The children are waiting to make snowballs
Snowflake, snowflake don't let us wait
We need to make our snowman and have fun with our skates

The joy you bring us when you are here
Remains in our memory throughout the year
So don't keep us waiting very long
Because we need you not in Heaven but on the ground.

Vinood Saroop (8)
Hambrough Primary School

WINTER

Snowflakes, cornflakes,
Fall from the sky,
Open your mouth and eat them high,
Icy ice,
Eat some pies,
Then wear some ties,
Ice says, snow flies,
Snow keeps it a secret
But snow cries
Sneeze, sneeze
All you want, not my fault,
Have big sleeves,
Please, please,
Everybody sneeze,
I want everybody to be
Sneezy, sick,
So I can have all the snow,
Ice-skating, ice-skating,
What a creating machine,
Whoosh!
Wind, are you going to date Blizzard?
You have so much in common.

Nikesh Gohil (9)
Hambrough Primary School

WINTER

Winter is cold,
It snows a lot,
So what!
Children love
Playing with such
Lovely snowflakes,
Snowflakes, snowflakes fall
From the sky
And play with them as fast as you can
And they will disappear

Winter, winter, why does it rain?
It rains so you can
Have fun, also
You can grow plants
To have oxygen or food
And to drink water
When it rains in winter
It gets frosty

Sometimes it's sunny
When it's sunny, I like it.

Ayat Mansab (9)
Hambrough Primary School

THE FAMILY

Ten adults going crazy
Nine children in bed
Eight grandmas in hospital
Seven babies crying
Six babies pulling people's hair

Five cousins crying
Four girls eating sweets
Three boys being lazy
Two children screaming
One mum getting fed up
And that's my mum.

Reshma Sharma (9)
Hambrough Primary School

CHOCOLATES

All my friend ever talks about is chocolates, chocolates
Always chocolates!
Never apples or even pears
Never fears or even gears
Never animals like bears
But always chocolates, chocolates
And even more chocolate!
I'm fed up of it!
Never maths or even science
Never school or even the pool
Never about geeks or streets
But always chocolates!
Never about drinks like Coke
Never about sprinters or even pinches
Never about himself or even me and Hermoine
He never, ever speaks about anything but chocolates!
And I'm fed up with it
Never about logic or even stories
Never about bullies like big fat Nelson
Or even different sorts of people
But always chocolates
I can't put up with it any longer.

Iqra Bhatti (9)
Hambrough Primary School

SAY TO YOURSELF EVERY MORNING . . .

Today is going to be a great day!
I can handle more than I think I can!
Things don't get better by worrying about them!
I can be satisfied if I try to do my best!
There is always something to be happy about!
Life is great, make the most of it,
Be an optimist!

Amarjit Chana (8)
Hambrough Primary School

SUN!

Sun! You're hot,
You shine on my face
And I get sunburnt,
Sun! You're so famous,
We have to wear shorts and a T-shirt
When you come out,
I love the sun.

Simran Gill (9)
Hambrough Primary School

MY FEAR

My fear is
When I am asleep
I have a dream
I think there are ghosts all around me

I put my head under my pillow and stay
There absolutely still, I get the shivers
And I am really scared, I think there is blood around me
So I just hide under my pillow.

Kimrit Marway (9)
Hambrough Primary School

IN THE PLAYGROUND

In the playground
There's always fighting going on
People cry and cry
It seems like five hundred people are
Crying and fighting
Only one boy is playing
I am going to see him
And smile.

Vishal Ehounhan (9)
Hambrough Primary School

THE SNOW

Snow is white
It is round
As a clock
I like snow
It is fun and as cold as the winter
Snow is like water
It's icy and slippery.

Geerthana Vigneswaran (9)
Hambrough Primary School

HALLOWE'EN IS TONIGHT

After school, my mum said,
'Clean up your closet!'
So I did.
When I went inside, I had . . .

One humungous green spider, weaving a web,
Two red-eyed mummies trying to wrap up their head,
Three vampires searching for rotten blood,
Four witches looking for solid trouble,
Five soggy socks trying to soak,
Six dead people, trying to help the socks,
I think I won't tidy my closet!

Karishma Fatania (8)
Hambrough Primary School

A DAY IN THE LIFE OF A TEACHER

Teacher wakes up
Goes to school
Tells people off
Goes on a break
Chats
Then tells more people off
Goes to lunch
Chats
Tells people off
Goes home
Talks to friends on the phone
Cooks dinner
Takes her aspirin
Goes to sleep.

Vanisha Bharadwa (8)
Hambrough Primary School

WHAT IS IT LIKE IN AFRICA?

What is it like in Africa?
I can see ribbons of colours skipping through the sky,
I can see the sun like a ball of fire.

What is it like in Africa?
I can hear the waves clashing and splashing together,
I can hear the joyful music of the African people.

What is it like in Africa?
I can feel my heart pounding faster and faster,
I can feel my worries flying out of my heart.

What is it like in Africa?
I can see the moon closing its eyes,
I can see the darkness tugging at my heart.

What is it like in Africa?
I can smell the sweet smell of candles,
I can smell the firewood of the fire.

Nia Acquaye (9)
Hayes Park Primary School

AFRICA

Me and my mum calmly watch the sunset go down,
Our worries just float away,
I close my eyes and smell the salty sea,
I hear the African tribal dancing and singing
Around the burning fire.
The sunset goes down calmly and humidly,
You ought to go to Africa,
It's getting dark.

Hayley Brimble (9)
Hayes Park Primary School

A SPECIAL ROOTS POEM

I am a root, rough and dry,
I am small and crooked, brown and cream,
I look like a tiny tree with millions of roots.
I drink lots of water and I used to be apart of a plant.
I smell of a beautiful flower, but I am very muddy too.
I am only a baby root, but I've come from a flower.

Abby Stokes (8)
Hayes Park Primary School

AFRICA

Fiery ashes in the sky,
Animals watch you as if there's a hidden mystery,
A scorching sunset blankets the sky.

Just imagine . . .
The humid breeze blows the soft sand around
The dusty desert.

Bhavinder Reyatt (8)
Hayes Park Primary School

AFRICA

A frica is a very hot country and very humid,
F ar out from the villages there is a wild jungle,
R oaring lions hunting for their prey,
I ce cream is a very nice treat for African people,
C ows eat the green juicy grass,
A frican people shout to get people's attention.

Daniel Dyer (9)
Hayes Park Primary School

THE RISING SUN

A frican sunset lights up the sky
F orever the sun rises
R ising sun opening its eyes at the top of the snow-capped mountains
I n the high mountains watching the sunrise
C an I touch the beaming sun?
A way the sun goes, closes his eyes at the bottom of the
                                                    dusky mountains.

Nicholas Everley (9)
Hayes Park Primary School

THE SUNSET

I can see the sunset
With all the dark colours around me,
The only sound I can hear are the birds singing in the distance,
I feel as calm as a leaf,
I feel easy and relaxed,
I could lie here forever,
I can smell the salty sea,
The sunset is fading,
I can't tell you anymore.

David Walker (8)
Hayes Park Primary School

UNTITLED

Warm colours stripe the sky,
Humid air strokes the ground,
Animals roam the scorching ground,
This is an African setting.

Daniel Rickwood (9)
Hayes Park Primary School

GOODNIGHT

Animals laying
Scorching in
The sun.

Elephants move the
Earth as they
Walk.

I see dusty monkeys
Jumping through the
Calm, tall trees.

Magnificent giraffes
Close their eyes.

The baking heat
Has made
Them tired.

Goodnight.

Alice Rose Shilling (8)
Hayes Park Primary School

AFRICA

A   frican tribes marching around angrily
F   ighting their enemies
R   efusing to stop fighting
I   mages beautiful, peaceful and bright
C   attle are gracefully eating the grass
A   nd then it turns to night and the sun closes its eyes.

Hannah Seers (8)
Hayes Park Primary School

AFRICA

The sun surrounds me as I run
Through the dusty, deserted desert.
The sun is tugging
At my skin,
It's like it's trying
To bite me and shrivel
Me up!
I feel like I can't get away,
I hear the roar of a cheetah,
But I don't see anything,
The land is so barren,
I scream
And walk into a zebra!
Argh!
I run the other way,
But it's too fast,
Then I stop . . .
It was just my imagination!

Francesca Browne (9)
Hayes Park Primary School

UNTITLED

Africa is a scorching place to live
And it has the best sunsets

Africa has joyful people who dance
And sing like pop stars in the swaying sky

Africa puts a light in your heart
I hope I can experience that light one day.

Max Corner (8)
Hayes Park Primary School

AFRICAN SUNSETS

Hi, this is my poem, so don't get too shy,
My heart is pounding so much
I can hardly breathe,
By the animals staring at me.

Night time is the time to be calm,
Steaming sun lightens the sky,
Elephants drooping over the land,
Animals walking over the land, with their perfect legs,
The scorching sunset says goodbye,
The sunset is fading away, that's all I've got to say.

Ifrah Rafique Nasseem (9)
Hayes Park Primary School

SUMMER SUNSET

Summer sunsets
Light up the sky,
You know it
Lies up high,
Nothing will beat
This big ball of
Blazing fire,
Summer sunsets don't
Get higher,
Elephants roam across the sky
Then they look up
And see the tiger's stripes,
This sunny bright light
Faded swiftly away.

Sian Forbes-White (9)
Hayes Park Primary School

THE AFRICAN SUN

A frica is really hot and an amazing place and it has a lovely
    hot blazing sunset
F ar out in our jungles are fierce, raging, wild animals
R aging sun boils you, it is like you are in an oven
I n Africa it is like you are on the scorching sun and you are melting
C aution, the sun is a blazing eye-blinding sun
A frica it is a quiet, peaceful and wonderful place.

Jake Louis Pulman (8)
Hayes Park Primary School

KENYA

My heart is thudding
It feels like the world is spinning
And the sun is wrapping itself around me like a ring
I'm unable to break free
The sun rapidly closing in on me
I feel like I'm in another world
I'm being tortured
Cracks from the Earth tearing open
A dark shadow overcomes the world
But suddenly a blade of light roars through the night
And it is defeated
And the beaming sun gets its revenge
The hearing of the red roaring sky burning out its power
The Earth is barren
As I walk away, slowly the sun calms down
And wanders off into the night.

Rahul Nisanth (9)
Hayes Park Primary School

MY AFRICAN SUNSET

My African sunset,
Scorching like the sun.

My African sunset
Is like a lion's face.

My African sunset,
Feels like my worries are blown away.

My African sunset
Is dusty and red-hot.

My African sunset
Is closing its eyes.

Jaskiran Virdee (8)
Hayes Park Primary School

THE SUN

In the horizon,
I am standing there,
Letting my feet burn into fire.
The sun is watching me
And won't stop,
Until I melt into flames.
The orange colours
Are too strong and bright,
I think I will turn blind or die.
Africa, you are a strong flame to me,
You are something strong,
Fierce and frightful,
Something that makes me feel
Hot and golden.

Michaela Pearce (9)
Hayes Park Primary School

AFRICA

I am standing on the scorching earth of Africa,
The sun is beaming down on my skin,
I raise my hand
And it's like putting my hand into red roaring fire,
Africa you are powerful.
The sun is ripping my soul out,
A shadow of darkness appears upon my head,
Everything goes quiet,
Suddenly,
A giant blade of light
Slashes through the dark shadow.
It's the sun, he's got his revenge,
Africa you are powerful.
It's light again, the sun is sparkling,
The desert is deserted,
As the sun roars to sleep,
Down it embers,
A glittering sunset,
Settles the night,
Africa you are powerful.

Josh Leighton (9)
Hayes Park Primary School

AFRICA!

A   frica is a raging hot place
F   ire is what the sun likes
R   hinoceroses grazing in the water
I   really like Africa, do you?
C   attles munching in the humid field
A   frica is a great place.

Bradley Clarke (8)
Hayes Park Primary School

THE SUN WINS

The sunset is warm and bright,
The dark, dusty shadows trying to bust their way in,
The sun is battling to keep the bright sun brighter,
The sun is trying to keep warm,
The dark trees trying to get the dark dusty shadows to win
But the sand is helping the sun and the sun wins.

Jordan Berry (9)
Hayes Park Primary School

THE TREE IN MY GARDEN

The tree in my garden is
As rusty as an old bin,
This tree is very dark,
It is bumpy and hard,
Oh, this tree it is as hard as a rock,
I wish I was that tree,
Standing there all day with
Leaves falling off the branches,
That's what I'll be,
I'll be a tree.

Lauren Mason (7)
Hayes Park Primary School

PINK BLOSSOM

It lies on trees and gets blown off by the wind,
It's cold and pretty and pink.
If I was that blossom, I would feel sad,
If I got blown away from everyone else.

I wish I was like it,
I would be always patterned.
I wish people would put me in water,
Instead of me dying.

Annie Jones (8)
Hayes Park Primary School

MR TWIG

He's prickly
He's tangled
He's rough
And he's hard
He's spiky all over
With a dull body
At night he gets longer
And really huge
He's really solid.

Dylan Saib (7)
Hayes Park Primary School

GREEN GRASS

Grass is green.
Grass is tall.
Grass is soft.
Grass is shiny.
Grass is calm.
Grass is blowing in the wind.
It is silent in the night.

Harlie Shelton (7)
Hayes Park Primary School

KENYA

All around is the sizzling sunset
As I stand in Africa
The red, roaring sky stands above me
The sun slowly fades away

It sparkles all day in the desert
It is our shining light that burns
It shines on the dancing Kenyan children

I walk into the light of the moon
As I walk into Kenya

The snake sizzles in the dark

Flames burn on me
The sun hits the floor
I hear the lions roar
I fade like the sparkling sun.

Charlotte Fairclough (8)
Hayes Park Primary School

MY TREE POEM

I am rough and bumpy
I have small holes
And lots of branches
I am brown and rough
My leaves are on the branches
I am stuck to soil
And I grow from seeds
I start from small
And I grow tall
What am I?

Karan Soni (8)
Hayes Park Primary School

KENYA

I am standing on the scorching desert
With a red-hot blanket
Flying over my head

I see the sun gently rising up
Into my eyes

I can smell the sandy, deserted desert
With little bits flying up my nose

I can feel the sun beating on me like a drum

I can hear the birds waking up
And singing in my ear.

Olivia Carpenter (9)
Hayes Park Primary School

THE MOON AND THE SUN

I am standing on the
Smashed Earth
Mashed by the powerful
Rays of the sun
But the moon battles
And leads a field of
Dark warriors
To darken the light
And win the sky
They still battle for the sky
On and on
Until one rules the sky
Forever.

Krish Pattni (9)
Hayes Park Primary School

AFRICA

All around is the sizzling sunset as I stand in Africa
I hear beautiful noises all around,
In the fields it teems with lions and all sorts
But actually I am in Africa
On the hot, burning floor
I see snakes and lions
I feel my body burning
Up to my toes
To my brain
Cracking in my toes and fingers
I smell people's sweat
In the hot beaming Africa
I also feel the touch of the hotness
Rising from the ground
It beats like my heart glazing in the hot sky.

Hannah Dignam (9)
Hayes Park Primary School

KENYA

As I am standing in a dry and dusty track,
The sun is blazing down on my face,
I cannot bear the sun,
Suddenly everything goes dark,
The sun has gone in behind a cloud,
I say, 'Phew,'
Then I start to run to the nearest tap
Because my water bottle is empty,
Then the sun comes out from behind the clouds,
Then I immediately stop and shield my eyes.

Sean Bruno (9)
Hayes Park Primary School

WHAT I FEEL, HEAR AND SEE IN KENYA

Inside my body I feel like
I'm burning like I'm on fire

And then I see the winter
Cold mountains looking at me
Telling me you can turn into
A big, yellow, orange sun

I see the red sky like blood
Telling me Jesus is rising again
And then I walk on the blazing
Hot, crackling ground and my feet go hot
And I feel like I'm in a pan sizzling like
I'm an egg and sausage baking
I'm in oil like a pancake

And then the sun is reflecting on me
Making me roast like a chicken

And I hear you say
Please don't make me burn like fire

And I see the sun scorching down
Like I never got this hot before

I see orange, red and yellow
In the sky, like God doesn't know
Which colour to put in the sky
And has just mixed the colours

And when I hear tigers roar
It makes me feel like it's been hunted
And it is in danger
I just wish that hunters weren't that mean.

Tiffany Yarde (8)
Hayes Park Primary School

SUNSET

I am walking along the sunset,
The sunset of Africa,
On the barren dry ground,
In a safari desert.

The sun is beaming down on me,
Ripping off all my skin,
Crackling the ground,
Like an earthquake on its way.

I can hear birds,
Flying around in the sky,
In the hot, boiling air,
Almost dying a death.

I can see trees,
Swaying in the breeze,
No leaves on it,
Maybe it's dead.

I can smell the hot air
And dust flying around me,
The sun gets hotter and hotter,
Trying to kill everyone.

I feel the sizzling sun,
Spreading to my face,
The ground is throwing me up,
In the boiling hot air.

I am standing in the middle of a desert,
Drinking a glass of water,
I am feeling really tired,
Of a long, long day.

I am walking along in the sunset,
The sunset of Africa.

Lauren Edwards (9)
Hayes Park Primary School

KENYA

The ground is tearing my feet up
And the cracking sun is beaming in my eyes
Trying to blind me
The sky is bright, fiery-red
Battling to take over the night
The heat is blistering hot.

George Painter (8)
Hayes Park Primary School

THE SUN

I'm standing on the hot scorching sun
I smell the dusty, rocky ground
I'm feeling as dizzy as a daisy
Hearing the sizzling of the sun
Like a powerful roaring engine
The night is blowing the heat away from me
I feel nice and cool in the breeze.

Amy Brown (8)
Hayes Park Primary School

KENYA

In the sweltering sun
Is where I stand
The sun is beaming down
Like a ray of light
It is blinding

The sun is too bright for me
I might die here
On this rocky road

The flames dry out this hard, barren land
Where the sun glitters and shimmers.

Tara Ludhra (9)
Hayes Park Primary School

KENYA

As the sun shines down on me
I roast up, the sky is as red as blood
It is two times hotter than England
When I move I burn up
So I can't move one bit
Because it is too hot.

Lacey Welter (8)
Hayes Park Primary School

AFRICA

I am standing on the ground
And the sun is in a bad rage
And the tremendous heat is biting me
Pinning me to the ground

All I can see is a deserted desert
And all the sweat running down me
Feels like a bucketful of hot water thrown over me
I can see the sunset fading away like embers.

Joe Chambers (9)
Hayes Park Primary School

KENYA

I am standing on the rough ground in Africa

I hear leaves
Dropping on the floor
In Africa

I hear guns shooting from
Five miles away
Bang! Bang! Bang!
At the wild animals
To save people's lives
I hope they're saved

I see a lion fighting a water hog
I don't want to look
There is a volcano dropping rocks

I smell fire burning
Finally I feel coldness hitting me as the sun
Escapes and the night slips down
I need to rest
But where?
Here's a tree.

Lewis Richards (9)
Hayes Park Primary School

AFRICA

The colours go wild around me,
In the sunset of Africa,
The straight black silhouettes creep behind you,
The sun dies slowly in the light of the evil moon,
As the ugly darkness grows,
People mourn for houses
To live in,
The sun rises and the deadly
Silhouettes fade into dust,
All is calm!
The land awakes,
Birds sing,
The sun is as bright as ever,
It beats with excitement,
The grass perks up from sleep,
The village begins to wake!
Babies cry,
Farms start work,
People get dressed for another day of life,
The animals wait for food,
Children wait for breakfast,
Schools prepare for the worst day of their lives,
Everyone is busy,
The day is over, the battle starts again,
The night is out to kill!

Chelsea Lauren Venier (9)
Hayes Park Primary School

AFRICA

I'm standing in the middle of Africa
And the sun is shimmering down my spine,
The sun is crackling on my skin,
I see a tribe hunting
In the distance,
Their masks are long,
They remind me of the mighty lion,
It is getting darker,
The sun is now down.

The sun is rising for another scorching day,
The day is getting hotter and hotter
As I wander on.

Charles Savin (8)
Hayes Park Primary School

KENYA

I am in a tropical setting
The golden sun is melting me
The ground is pulling me down
Into a black hole
I hear rustling in the grass
And prowling, it's a lion
My heart is beating so frantically
I cannot think now
The sun is going
The moon is coming up
It's all black
Africa, you are too strong for me.

Bianca-Nicole Knott
Hayes Park Primary School

KENYA

I feel the sun pricking my skin in the hot African desert
I see the sunset, I look at it as if it was a blob of paint in the sky
I hear the sizzling sun burning the hot African ground
I smell the burning sunlight in the sky reflecting down on me
The sun tears me in half with its burning blaze.

Ryan Brennand (8)
Hayes Park Primary School

THE TROJAN HORSE

The Greeks set sail out to sea
For at Troy a battle there be

They tried to use the battering ram
It didn't work, so they thought of a plan

They built a big wooden horse
The Trojans pulled it in with brute force

For in the house their soldiers be
The Greeks killed them silently

They rescued Helen up in the tower
King Menelaus bought her a flower

The Greeks decided to loot the city
A leftover Trojan thought, *what a pity*

The Greeks set sail back home
Where their wives were all alone.

Connor Orton (10)
Laleham CE Primary School

SNOW POEM

Your face remains crisp and white,
I love the way you look,
I always wait till you come,
Oh snow, oh snow,
You're like an open book,
You're always fun to play with,
Nobody doubts that,
But I have to prepare to be with you,
Put on my gloves and hat,
I hope you're here today,
My very best friend,
I love it when you come,
But hate it when you end,
But still your face remains crisp and white,
I love the way you look!

Lucy Wood-Ives (11)
Laleham CE Primary School

NIGHT

Night moves slowly through the air,
Silently, silently,
She is unpredictable, mysterious,
Her glowing red eyes float around creepily,
While her rasping breath rattles out of her cold and cut mouth,
She tosses her tangled hair back,
Whirls around, dragging her black cloth behind her,
As she blinds me with her blackness.

Eleanor Mitchell (10)
Laleham CE Primary School

POCKETS

What's inside our pockets?
To most people it brings joy
A squashed-up packet of chewing gum
A penny or maybe a toy

But in my pocket it's a different matter
An experimenting lizard
A wand, a quill and a bottle of ink -
Because I, of course, am a *wizard.*

Rose Chittenden (8)
Laleham CE Primary School

STARS

Stars light up the night
They glow and gleam like diamonds
They're small or big
But normally small
They lead the way for travellers
Passing through the night
Some stars shoot across the night
While others stay still
There's always one brighter
Than the rest
To make your wish come true.

Lauren Hedges (10)
Laleham CE Primary School

THE GOD OF WINTER

The god of winter
Sits on his throne with his slaves at his side
The god of winter is trying to think of what hat and scarf to buy
He is preparing for his special winter spell
He finally decides what he will wear
He smiles with his blue lips, saying he looks good

The slaves speak up saying to their master
'You better hurry up.'
The god of winter puts on his hat and scarf
As he walks over to the wintry sky
He says the magic words
And *boom* there is a flash of light
The god of winter has made it snow
'Oh the joy of winter,' the slaves croak.

Tamsyn Hedges (10)
Laleham CE Primary School

NIGHT

Night is a dark man
And creeps around
In black robes and
Is lonely and always
Around you, ready to
Get you as he covers
The world in darkness
Ready for me and you
Till the dawn, until
Light appears again.

Nicola Maple (10)
Laleham CE Primary School

WINTER QUEEN

As the winter queen is coming,
Everyone is getting ready,
Look at her, she's settling on the ground,
She makes everyone walk over her white tummy.

She hears the joy,
She breathes out into the air,
The other kids get cold but she doesn't care,
Her feet are white and cold under my feet.

When I have to go home for tea,
I don't want to leave my best friend,
The winter queen.

The winter queen isn't always there,
But who cares?
I've got other friends in my life.

I'll be waiting until the next winter comes,
But what if she doesn't come as well?
Oh well, I'll play with my other friends.

As the winter queen is coming,
Everyone is getting ready,
Look at her, she's settling on the ground,
She's making everyone walk over her white tummy.

Kiri Gibson (10)
Laleham CE Primary School

QUEEN OF MOONLIGHT

When night comes
She appears dressed in white
Scaring away all fears

Her dress tight around her slender hips
Haltered to see her twilight feet
Her hair flowing down to her fingertips
In waves of golden sea

She walks over the world
In time for night
Her eyes shining bright like stars

A band lay gently upon her head
Studded in diamonds
Reassuring them
She is the queen of moonlight

When night comes
She appears dressed in white
Scaring away all fears

Her face just as pretty as her heart
Kind and loving
Which awakens the night sky

She is the queen of moonlight
Brightening the sky for you and me
She'll be here for you when there's
Nobody there to see.

Emma Waite (11)
Laleham CE Primary School

MY COOL BEYBLADE

Beyblades are fun,
Beyblades are round,
I like to play with them
In the playground

Beyblades are fun,
Beyblades are great,
I like to play with them
On my gate.

Beyblades are fun,
They sing and dance,
They even have me in
An hypnotised trance.

Beyblades are fun,
Beyblades are cool,
I even like them
In the swimming pool.

Simon Spencer (9)
Lyon Park Junior School

WIND

A door slammer
An umbrella wrecker
A hat stealer
A dustbin thief
A window rattler
A leaves rustler
Who am I?

Varusni Premabala (8)
Lyon Park Junior School

SEASONS

Summer days we swim for fun
Springtime we love eating buns
Winter days freezing but enjoyable
Autumn time we get playful

Summer days out in the streets
Springtime stamping feet
Winter days sitting by the fire
Autumn time winds sing like a choir

Summer days by the sea
Springtime busy as a bee
Winter days you will get a cold
Autumn time you'll be bold

Summer days spent at home
Springtime we get a loan
Winter days quickly get inside
Autumn time play on slides.

Meeta Dattani (9)
Lyon Park Junior School

THE NOISY WOODPECKER

The woodpecker is a driller
It makes holes in the trees
And annoys the bees
The bees come out
And play about
'Go away!'
The woodpecker shouts!

Rohini Patel (8)
Lyon Park Junior School

WEATHER

The weather is sunny
And I am playing with my bunny
The weather is cold
But I am making a teddy with my mould
The weather is bad
And I am going mad
The weather is rainy
But I am brainy
It is snowing
And the sun is glowing
The weather is windy
And I like to play with my Sindy.

Luxshajine Kumaradevan (8)
Lyon Park Junior School

WIND KENNING

A paper taker
A hat stealer
A clothes stealer
A curtain mover
A window rattler
A ribbon taker
A branch sawyer
A bag flier
A leaf shaker
What am I?

Lychelle Christian (8)
Lyon Park Junior School

MY WHY, WHY POEM

Why, why do we shoot a gun?
Why, why do we never learn?
Why, why do we eat a bun?

Why, why don't we sing along?
Why, why do people get upset?
Why, why must we sing a song?

Why, why does it have to rain?
Why, why do people play?
Why, why don't people take
A ride on a train?

Why, why is the river low?
Why, why do we swim in a river?
Why, why do you say so?

Akshay Patel (9)
Lyon Park Junior School

PALM TREE

Growing little coconuts,
Swaying in the breeze,
On a little island,
In the big, big sea.
On this little island,
Right out in the sea,
Stands a little palm tree,
On a small, small island,
In a big, big sea,
In the big, big ocean,
Away from you and me.

Azfar Shafi (10)
Lyon Park Junior School

MY PET FISH

My pet fish,
  Swimming round and round.
My pet fish,
  Sitting on the ground.
My pet fish,
  Staring off to space.
My pet fish,
  Has a small drooping face.
My pet fish,
  Doesn't know what to do.
My pet fish,
  Has no family too.
My pet fish,
  Needs a family of its own.
My pet fish,
  He's all alone.
My pet fish,
  Gone forever and ever.
My pet fish,
  Never comes back, never.
My pet fish,
  Lying on the ground.
My pet fish,
  Never swims around.

Rahib Tarafder (9)
Lyon Park Junior School

FLYING

I smell breakfast,
I hear birds singing,
I feel the wind through my hair,
I smell freshly mowed grass,
I think, *why can't I stay up any longer?*

I smell the sweet air,
I hear children playing,
I feel the sunshine on me,
I smell the flowers,
I think, *why can't I stay up any longer?*

Pratibha Maharjan (10)
Lyon Park Junior School

WEATHER

When it's hot
I see the sun
Shining around
The place

When it's windy
It gives us speed
And makes it feel
Cold indeed

When it's rainy
There's nothing to do
And nowhere to go

When it's snowing
My face is glowing
The snow falls like a
Feather and it's soft
Like leather

There is nothing to do
On a rainy morning
Three is lots to do
On a sunny morning.

Milica Maksimovic (8)
Lyon Park Junior School

THE WEATHER

The weather is bright
The weather is dark
The sun is bright but more light
When it's dark
It's not so bright because it's night
The sun is yellow
But the moon is white
The children think it's funny
Because it's sunny
The dogs might bark
Because it's dark
The mice will play
Hide and squeak
And they might peek.

Keval Vyas (8)
Lyon Park Junior School

MY DREAM!

In my dream
I was driving a Ferrari
In the Italian Grand Prix
I was storming around the circuit
And I was beating Michael Schumacher
There was the line, I was near the line
I was approaching it fast
The car went out of control
The car exploded
The crowd thought I was dead . . .
But I jumped out my bed!

Miles Fearon (8)
Lyon Park Junior School

THE HAUNTED HOUSE

The house was empty, the house was dead!
The house was filled with human heads.

It had ghouls, zombies and even some skeletons
And worst of all, a human-eating Geloton.

Now what do you think this house was called?
It was the Haunted House of old man Macoy.

Macoy was vicious, Macoy was mad,
When Macoy was a boy, he was bad.

When you looked in his eyes, you would turn to stone
And he would then smile and eat your bones.

Ramone Phillips (10)
Lyon Park Junior School

MY FLIGHT WITH OWLS

Faster and faster
Now higher, now lower
Between evening trees
Through the starry midnight sky
Gliding through the big clouds
Rising above the city sounds
As straight as an arrow
I hovered and darted
Between the moon and stars
Whirling and twirling
Skimming the treetops
Hard and high
I flew with magnificent owls.

Aatikah Hayat (9)
Lyon Park Junior School

FLYING

As I flew in the sky,
I could smell the baking of bread,
The whooshing wind in my hair
And I saw the tops of people's heads.

I could hear the motor of a car
And thought, what if I can't stop flying
And I go so far?

I could feel the fresh air in my face
And I saw children having a running race.

Tasmiah Shiraz (10)
Lyon Park Junior School

ALL ABOUT ME

I am kind
But I have an awful mind
I have a head
Which is the colour of red

My favourite food is noodles
The worst animal you can look at is a poodle
I like snow
Because it makes me glow

My worst colour is green
But I wish to be a queen
My aunty is like a beam
That's why my worst colour's green.

Sherikah Paskaran (8)
Lyon Park Junior School

AN ALLITERATION POEM

Bossy Betty buried bones in Britannia
Choco Charlie sells chocolate in China
Danny Dingo dances like a dumb dodo
Emma Emu eats eggs every evening
Flori Frank finds famous film stars
Holli Hani has a hairy hand
Irene Ingo built an igloo on an island
Kelly Kate flew a kite with a kangaroo
Moany Mary moaned about mini meat pies
Oliver Oye always says 'Oi' in autumn.

Rehma Shaikh (10)
Lyon Park Junior School

SNOW

Snow so cold,
Icy and frosty,
It freezes ice
And rivers too!
People slide, slip
And glide,
It's watery, foggy
And sloppy as well,
Snow makes people
Slither, skid and shiver,
It drizzles, it's damp
And frosty,
The roads are frozen
And glacial too!

Kirsty Guy (9)
Lyon Park Junior School

DINOSAURS

Dinosaurs lived on this Earth long ago
They hunted in a place called old Chicago!

Dinosaurs came in all shapes and sizes
From far and wide to hide their prizes

Which they won for the most ugliest creatures
With horns and scales and so many strange features

Their skin was as rough as the sand on a beach
Some of their skin was the colour of a peach

Leaf-eating herbivores, flesh-eating carnivores
With sharp claws, big teeth and loud echoing roars.

Sejal Anujah Shah (10)
Lyon Park Junior School

SNOW

Soft, fluffy, cold snow
Landing on the trees,
Like a world covered in cotton wool,
White ice cream on a cone,
Icy, cold snow

Like popcorn tumbling from a bowl
Snow,
   Falling,
      Falling
         Falling . . .

Marin Daley-Hawkins (9)
Lyon Park Junior School

THE DAY I MET THE PRESIDENT

The day I met the President
Was seriously cool
We strolled around his garden
And we even had a duel

The day I met the President
Was simply fun
We had a game of darts
And guess what? I won

The day I met the President
Was such a great surprise
I spent the night at the Whitehouse
And we watched the sun rise

The day I met the President
I was too shy to say hello
I had such a supreme time
But now I have to go.

Sophie-Leigh Ali (9)
Lyon Park Junior School

THE OLD MAN FROM SPAIN

There was an old man from Spain
Who got here in a very big plane
He got mad
With his dad
And his dad thought he was insane.

Jathepan Chandrajah (9)
Lyon Park Junior School

My Room

In my room I have . . .

10 elephants that live in my wardrobe,
9 monkeys that swing on the light,
8 rabbits that live under the bed,
7 pigs that roll everywhere,
6 cats that drink my milk,
5 donkeys that eat my carpet,
4 snakes that slither about,
3 fish that live in the tank,
2 dogs that bark ever so loudly
And only one of me.

Dipti Bhudia (9)
Lyon Park Junior School

I Believe

I believe everybody is important
I believe we can live together
I believe if we care for each other
I believe we could live forever
I believe if everyone was happy
I believe if people were to share
Then I believe the world would care.

Yasin Mohammed (9)
Lyon Park Junior School

Valentine's Day

The sky is blue,
The fields are green,
Like my sweet baboon,
That's you.

Roses are red,
Violets are blue,
Love's in the air,
Just like you.

Hamel Premgi (10)
Lyon Park Junior School

I AM...

I am the song that the birds sing
I am the leaf that grows on the trees
I am the tide that comes in at night
I am the sand that sits near the sea
I am the cloud that works with the breeze
I am the sun that lights the Earth
I am the fire that burns from the start
I am who you want me to be.

Bhavik Varsani (10)
Lyon Park Junior School

VALENTINE'S DAY

Valentine's Day, Valentine's Day,
Roses are red,
Valentine's Day, love is always in the air,
Boys love girls,
Girls love boys,
Valentine's Day, love is here,
Love is there,
Love is everywhere.

Henna Haria (9)
Lyon Park Junior School

MY WORLD

If this world was mine,
I'd make the sun shine,
Through the trees and on the seas,
If this world was mine.

If this world was mine,
Everything would be just fine,
No more fights,
Lots of pretty sights,
If this world was mine.

If this world was mine,
There would be no crime,
No more pollution,
Only solution,
If this world was mine.

If this world was mine,
At this given time,
They'd be plenty to eat,
Proper clothes and enough sleep,
If this world was mine.

Louise Clack (9)
Lyon Park Junior School

ALIEN

A   is for aliens
L   is for lunar
I   is for invading Earth
E   is for entering the solar system
N   is for Neptune, their home.

Bina Patel (9)
Lyon Park Junior School

IF I COULD FLY

If I could fly
I would go to the sun to spend my holidays
If I could fly
I would go to outer space to share all my secrets with all the planets
If I could fly
I would go to Heaven and rest in peace
If I could fly
I would go to all the planets and taste the wonderful food
If I could fly
I would go to Mars, to sleep over on the planet
And the aliens could read me a bedtime story.

Pratik Patel (9)
Lyon Park Junior School

I'M SO ANGRY

I'm so angry
I could break my mum and dad's bedroom window
Why?
Because I got grounded for two weeks

I'm so sad
I could burst into tears
Why?
Because I got bullied at school

I'm so happy
I could pay for my mum and dad's window
Why?
Because I should not have done it in the first place.

Chevaunne Marney (9)
Lyon Park Junior School

THE COW

The friendly cow all red and white,
I love with all my heart,
She gives me cream with all her might,
To eat with apple tart.

She wanders, lowing here and there
And yet she cannot stray,
All in the pleasant open air,
The pleasant light of day.

Blown by all the winds that pass
And wet with all the showers,
She walks among the meadow's grass
And eats the meadow's flowers.

Sanjay Solanki (10)
Lyon Park Junior School

DOLPHIN

The cute baby dolphin
Is very mature
It loves to swim
It's a wonderful creature
The dolphin is very playful
It's full of happiness
It is blue and beautiful
It's also full of kindness
The dolphin makes a lovely sound
It has a lovely cute smile
The sound can be loud
It can swim for miles.

Varishma Assani (8)
Lyon Park Junior School

SPRING

I saw a flower,
It had lots of power.
A possum,
Smelled the blossom.
The raise of the sun,
Shone over my bun.
The scented gel,
Gave a nice smell.
Flowers glowed purple, yellow and orange,
Which reflected on my half-eaten orange.
There was pollen in the air,
But the people didn't care.
There were bees busy,
That made me dizzy.
They made sweet honey
That I could pour over my chocolate bunny.
There were lots of butterflies in the way
And some flew away.

Dina Solanki (8)
Lyon Park Junior School

POET IN SPACE

Space is like a world full of darkness
And circles that are multicoloured

It is as dark as night covering the whole world

It is as silent as the wind blowing
Through the air

It is as mysterious as a ghost
Roaming through the night.

Hiral Dani (9)
Lyon Park Junior School

VALENTINE'S DAY

Chocolates and flowers are all the craze,
Red hearts are everywhere around town,
Some find love in the Tunnel of Love,
Hugs and kisses all around,
It is a time of romance,
To show someone that you care,
You don't need flash things to impress,
Just show them that you care,
Even though you're poor,
Doesn't mean you can't have a Valentine,
It is a time to share,
No need for hundreds of pounds,
Red roses are taking over,
Cards are too,
It's no work and all play,
But overnight you become one more step closer to being perfect,
Next day you feel cheerier than ever,
But it's all work and no play,
Just show someone you care,
If you really like them,
You'll get closer each day,
Just around the corner,
Could be your best dream granted yet,
Or it could just be another mirage,
All you have to do is wait . . .

Suraj Padhiar (10)
Lyon Park Junior School

IF I HAD WINGS

If I had wings
I would touch the moon
Just gazing at it all night
Then when it is morning, I will see it soon

If I had wings
I would slide on the icy rings of Jupiter
Until I go dizzy
Then I just knew Gameboy was dead
So I needed an adaptor.

Dhilan Shivji (9)
Lyon Park Junior School

SNOW

Snow so bright
You glow in the night
You're the star of the twinkling light
Snow is crusty, snow is great
More than Heaven, I would give it an eight
Snow is not like white bits of litter
It is like shining glitter
Snow melts away in my hand
Snow is something everyone can stand
Snow is like white bits that fly
It is like diamonds lost in the night sky
Snow is the shimmer in your eye.

Serena Hussain (8)
Lyon Park Junior School

THE STRONG MAN

The strong man with big muscles
He fights like a bear
With fat hands
And strong as an ox.

Francisco Silva (9)
Lyon Park Junior School

ALL ABOUT ME

I love watching telly
In Year 3 I had a teacher called Mr Kelly
But he did not have a round belly

I have been to Hollywood
But never have been to Bollywood
That is jolly good

I like ringing bells
But I don't smell

I have a clever mind
And my friends are sometimes kind

My favourite colour is red
That's why I have a head

I hate cars
And have not been to Mars.

Karishma Patel (8)
Lyon Park Junior School

THINK OF ALL THE DAYS

Sunny and bright on Sunday
Moany and might on Monday
Tummy and tight on Tuesday
Windy and night on Wednesday
Tidy and light on Thursday
Funny and fright on Friday
Shiny and right on Saturday
Think of all the days of the week
They are sunny and bright.

Logini Saththiyan (8)
Lyon Park Junior School

ANIMALS

I love my cat
Well fancy that
And I like mice
I think they're nice
Some dogs are scruffy
And some are fluffy
Rabbits are shy
But they cannot fly
Fish are scaly
And have big tailies
Snakes are scary
But are not hairy
Elephants are wrinkly
And feel all crinkly
Giraffes are tall
But to them we're small
Lions are fierce
And like to pierce
Crocodiles are snappy
When they are happy
Monkeys are cheeky
When they are sneaky
Dolphins are grey
And play all day
Bears like honey
But have no money
Owls have big eyes
And fly though night skies
I'd like to be a vet
But I'm not old enough yet.

Jasmine Bird (9)
Lyon Park Junior School

QUICKLY AND QUIETLY

Quickly the rocket
blasts off into space

Quietly the worm wriggles
through a hole

Quickly the cheetah
leaps through the jungle

Quietly I slept
in my bed!

Adam Minhas (9)
Lyon Park Junior School

SLOWLY AND SILENTLY

Slowly the mouse nibbled the cheese
Silently the cat walked into the kitchen
Slowly the river flooded the land
Silently the boy rested on his bed.

Henay Bhuva (8)
Lyon Park Junior School

NO TREES!

Never seeing emerald leaves
Never hearing the rustling of leaves
No home for the lovely tweeting birds
No place for insects to climb up
Nowhere to get oxygen from.

Miriam Belaid (8)
Lyon Park Junior School

MACHINES INTO ANIMALS

The woodpecker is a screwdriver
It makes holes in trees

The train is a snake
It goes up and down and slithers

The crocodile is a hole pincher
It makes holes in paper or your skin.

Vishal Kothari (8)
Lyon Park Junior School

BUTTERFLY

Butterflies are small,
But they cannot crawl,
Butterflies eat worms,
Every summer
Butterflies fly high,
Right in the sky.

Sarah Hanif (9)
Lyon Park Junior School

CATS

Cats are cute
Cats are nice
Cats are white
Cats are black
Some are fat
And some are thin
Cats lick their bodies.

Needa Iqbal (8)
Lyon Park Junior School

THE COLD CAT

There once was a cat that looked quite fat.

His fur looked mouldy
And he always moaned and groaned.

His name was Pat Gold
And he always felt very old.

Pat the cat hasn't got a home,
That's why Pat's mat is cold.

Poor old cat,
Got a cold mat.

All he wants is a home!

Ashley Hassan (8)
Lyon Park Junior School

DINOSAURS

Dinosaurs run around,
Eating trees and leaves,
Wheat and meat.
Creatures very tough,
Lost in a world of their own.
Hurting, killing,
It shouldn't have been like that.
Sadly extinct, 2,000,000 years ago.
Why did they fight?
Why did they bite?
Why was it the way it was?
Why? Why? Why?

Hassan Akram-Sheikh (9)
Lyon Park Junior School

WEATHER

The weather can be good,
the weather can be bad,
it can be sad.

I was thinking to go outside,
but thought I would get wet,
even though I've got a raincoat.

But then a beautiful rainbow came
and a shining sun, *yippee!*
Now we can play outside
and all the tension of homework is out of your mind.

Now it's bright,
you don't need lights,
it will be dark late because summer is here.

Tomorrow is school,
I finished my homework
and hope that it is sunny,
    best of luck!

Richa Desai (9)
Lyon Park Junior School

THE BOY FROM GREECE

There was a boy from Greece
Who from a sheep stole a fleece
Who drank some wine
And bought a sign
Then he had a lot of peace!

Ashit Mamtora (9)
Lyon Park Junior School

CHRISTMAS

C   hurch bells go *dong*
H   oliday for Christians
R   ed-nosed reindeer flies in the sky
I   enjoy Christmas
S   ilver starts shining in the sky
T   all Christmas tree, beautifully decorated
M   ary gave birth to Jesus Christ
A   ngels singing songs
S   anta coming to give presents to us
    This is what I call Christmas!

Khyati Alpesh Patel (10)
Lyon Park Junior School

THE SUNRISE

Early in the morning
The break of dawn
The gleaming sun sprinkles on
My lawn
The copper sun shines upon me
I lie in bed too blind to see
As the sun goes high
Up in the sky
The aeroplanes and birds
Going to fly
Birds are chirping
Bees are buzzing
It's a new day
Which will bring lots of
Surprises.

Pavan Panesar (10)
North Primary School

THE YELLOW LADY!

A yellow lady walking by a stream
I'm wondering what is her dream?
A little bird jumps from her heart
'I say what a cute bird.'
Come on, come on, I'll show you how
You come with me and you will see
Your eyes light up with wonderful glee
A yellow lady walking by a stream
I'm wondering what is her dream?
I walk further down and I see something brown
What is it? What is it?
Pinewood it is
If you're feeling all sad and blue
Come with me and you'll be happy.

Samira Sidhu (8)
North Primary School

A PINK BUTTERFLY

It emerges from its cocoon,
Freeing its wings into mid-air,
It flutters rapidly,
Shimmering in the light.
It spreads its wings,
Far beyond the horizon.
It's like a sparkle in your eye,
It glistens against the sun.
Its wings close like curtains,
Then it's time to say goodbye
And rejoin the family.

Jemini Gova (11)
North Primary School

AND SHE WAS GONE

There is a girl on the street
Walking in the night
Terrified and lonely
And then she saw a light

She runs to the light
As fast as she could
Running like a cheetah
And there she stood

She couldn't move her legs
And there stood a light glowing
Right in front of her eyes
Then came a gust of wind blowing

She ran in the light
In her eyes was the light that shone
She went deeper and deeper
And there she was gone.

Aisha Iqbal (10)
North Primary School

THE EVERLASTING SNOW

No breath of wind
No gleam of sun
Still the white snow
Whirls softly down
Twig and bough
And blade and thorn
All in an icy, quiet, forlorn
Whispering, rustling
Through the air
On still and stone
Roof - everywhere

It leaps its powdery
Crystal flakes
Of every tree
A mountain makes;
Till pale and faint
At shut of day
Stops from the west
One wintry ray
And feathered in fire
Where ghosts the moon
A robin shrills
His lonely tune . . .

Sangeeta Saundh (11)
North Primary School

GOLD

Gold! Gold! Gold!
Gold is beautiful
Gold is funny
Gold is a bunny
Gold is sunny
Gold is a honey
Gold is lovely
Gold is a mountain
Gold is a fountain
Gold! Gold! Gold!
It's my favourite colour.

Tarunveer Lochan (9)
Norwood Green Junior School

I Wish...

I wish that I was a dolphin swimming in the ocean,
I wish that I was a fish dancing in the sea,
I wish that I was a sea travelling around the world,
I wish that I was like you, like you, like you,
I wish I was a rich girl,
I wish I was a beautiful girl,
I wish I was a star looking at people below me,
I wish that I was a bird singing all day, all day, all day,
I wish that I was a beautiful, colourful, pretty, feathery peacock.
I wish that my wish came true.

Shruthi Narayana (10)
Norwood Green Junior School

My Football Hero

I have many football heroes
Some short, some tall
Some good, some bad
Some fat, some thin
But they'll all be my favourite.
Some from England, some from France
Some from Brazil, some from Germany
Some from Spain, some from Italy
But they'll all be my favourite.
Some play for Liverpool, some play for Arsenal
Some play for Chelsea, some play for Newcastle
Some play for Roma, some play for Real Madrid
But they'll all be my favourite.
Now you know some of my favourites you'll know
That I am a football fan, hope you are too.

Amit Chhoker (9)
Norwood Green Junior School

CHOCOLATE

Chocolate swirling rivers,
Chocolate blossoming flowers,
Chocolate mint soft grass,
Chocolate sweet, tasty fruit,
Chocolate schools,
Chocolate houses,
Yummy, delicious, original chocolate.

No chocolate swirling rivers,
No chocolate blossoming flowers,
No chocoloate mint soft grass,
No chocolate sweet, tasty fruit,
No chocolate schools,
No chocolate houses,
No yummy sweet, original chocolate,
Because . . . *it's in my belly!*

Gurphavan Kaur Sekhon (9)
Norwood Green Junior School

WIND

The wind is really cold
That makes me shiver all around
It blows me afar
So I run for safety
The faster I run
The colder I get
When I find shelter
I'll be better.

Kevin Mandalia (9)
Norwood Green Junior School

THE SOFT SWISH SEA

It's the same colour as the sky,
Where all of the birds fly,
What is it?
It's the soft swish sea!

It's the same colour as Dad's car,
That can drive very far,
What is it?
It's the soft swish sea.

It's the same colour as my door,
That swings across the floor,
What is it?
It's the soft swish sea.

It's the same colour as my wall,
That is very tall,
What is it?
It's the soft swish sea.

It's the same colour as all of these things,
It's blue and
What is it?
It's the soft swish sea.

Laura J Lynam (10)
Norwood Green Junior School

THE WIND

The wind is soft as a comfortable cushion
It flows through my hair
I try to catch it but I can't
It goes through my hand
The wind is everywhere

I can hear it whistling through my ear
But it goes through the other one
It swirls and curls everywhere
I wish I was the gleaming wind
That swirls and curls everywhere.

Bhawanjot Kaur Guron (10)
Norwood Green Junior School

POTTY ABOUT CHOCOLATE

Children love chocolate
And I'm no exception
I started eating it
When I was in reception
I sneaked into the classroom
When no one was around
I couldn't believe my eyes
Do you know what I found?
A whole bar of Aero
Begging me to have a bite
I didn't waste a second
I didn't put up a fight
I ate the Aero in one go
All of a sudden I started to choke

What am I talking about?
Ignore all that, the main thing is - chocolate makes you fat!
It ruins your teeth and makes you spotty
But in spite of all this, I'm still potty . . .
About chocolate!

Nicola Anne Piggott (9)
Norwood Green Junior School

ICE CREAM

Everyone likes ice cream, even parents
It's good for summer
But not for winter
It's smooth and delicate
But the bad thing is, it melts
Melt, melt, melt.

The flavours are vanilla, strawberry and so on
My favourite is chocolate
Do you like it?
I think so.

But really I like anything
Oh wait
The supermarket's about to close
And I need some ice cream
Got to buy some
Bye then.

Arvinder Sarai (9)
Norwood Green Junior School

HEAVEN

Heaven
The most peaceful place ever
Angels singing so sweet you'll be tired
There you will be with your family
And even happier
People having a great laugh over stuff.

Heaven
The most popular place ever
The most biggest place ever
Even! The most colourful place with roses
In several gardens.

Heaven
Almost every celebrity will be seen
Doing shopping or stuff
And the sunniest place ever to be seen
And people sunbathing.

Hamza Lakhanpal (10)
Norwood Green Junior School

NATURE

The mountain's spirit runs wildly, silently
through the trees as the great tongue
of blue
whispers
whispers
whispers
as the great tongue of blue whispers
to its soulmate the cliffs of the north.

The moon gloats for
hours
hours
hours
the moon gloats for hours
admiring his silver portrait on top
of the water's edge.

The whales call their
songs
songs
songs
the whales call their songs
as peace gallops through the night.

Zôe Connell (10)
Norwood Green Junior School

SNOW!

The snow came down gladly
As the snow came down rapidly
It poured and poured and poured

Crunch, crunch, crunch
The snow went
As the children run around

I looked back
A snowball hits me
I felt the snow
It was freezing cold

The chilled snow
Attacked my spine
As it slowly melted

Then the snow stopped
There was sorrow
Everyone went back to their homes.

Gurpreet Bains (10)
Norwood Green Junior School

FOOTBALL

The whistle's just gone off
Players getting ready
Everybody's shouting
Just be steady!

Owen's got the ball
But not very tall
About to score a goal
When Barthez saves the ball.

Anneeka Basra (9)
Norwood Green Junior School

AN ODE TO CHOCOLATE

Oh delicious chocolate
I adore your dark or light colours
Your different shapes and sizes take me one step closer to Heaven
As soon as I take one bite it makes me have the entire chocolate
in two huge gulps
I love the way you melt in my watery mouth
You are so sweet
My favourite one of you is Dairy Milk
I have it about five times a week
You're soft, bubbly inside is so enchanting
I treasure you greatly
If I get a box of chocolate I keep for myself
Unless I'm feeling generous.

Zehra Saifuddin (10)
Reddiford School

A HOLY WATER BOTTLE

She stands there as still as a statue
Her eyes closed and hands together praying for hope
Her sky and pale blue hat is like the Statue of Liberty
She wears the finest texture of clothes
She has an elongated necklace that is made of golden beads
Her clothes are almost like a sari
When you touch her you feel a soothing and peaceful feeling
She makes you feel more holy and calm
She looks extremely enchanting
All her clothes, glorious and fantastic, go in the same directions.

Conor O'Brien (9)
Reddiford School

FEELINGS

I'm feeling happy,
I'm feeling yellow.
Everything today
Seems so great and mellow.

I'm feeling sad,
I'm feeling blue.
Everyone today
Seems to be sad too.

I'm feeling jealous,
I'm feeling green.
Everything today
Seems so, so, so mean.

I'm feeling angry,
I'm feeling red.
Everything today
Seems to get to my head.

I'm feeling loving,
I'm feeling pink.
Everything today
Seems so loving too, I think.

I'm feeling scared,
I'm feeling black.
Everything today
Seems so very dark.

I'm feeling pure,
I'm feeling white.
Everything today
Seems to shine in light.

But now I'm feeling great,
Now I'm feeling golden!

Tejuswi Patel (10)
Reddiford School

SCHOOL

I go to a very big school
Many people think it's cool
Because we have a very big swimming pool
Where all the children are disciplined with no rule

Harry thinks he's too cool
For this place he calls school
Simon seems to like to drool
And my maths teacher is very cruel

She gives us homework all the time
Which in my opinion is a crime
Sometimes her behaviour can be very nice
Which she selects by throwing a dice

Sadly not everyone who goes to school is cool
There are big bullies who hits us with a tool
The teachers don't like that so they sit on a stool
With a big hat saying fool!

Kishan Ragunathan (9)
Reddiford School

GOCO THE COCONUT MONSTER

Goco the coconut monster
Lives in an island
Far from his family
And has no friends.

He is huge
Bigger than anything you have seen
Eats fish and honey
And drinks water.

He has a big long tail
And mean eyes
Bushy eyebrows
And he is very fierce.

He has a big fat body
Long hairy legs
And thin
He also has black shoes.

He has dangling ears
He can hear everything
He can talk
And he laughs so loudly.

He has long arms
His hands have fat fingers
And he has three lines, which are marks
He has even got sharp teeth.

He lies around under the coconut trees
Eating coconut
Sleeping and dreaming of his family
He always scares people.

He gets annoyed if people come near him
If they do he bites them.

Roshni Adatia (9)
Reddiford School

TORNADO

Swirling, swishing faster than light,
The tornado thunders throughout the night.
Torrential winds flood the plain,
People living there experience pain.

Absorbing everything in its way,
The cyclone brings a wicked day.
Houses, trees everything around,
The tornado attacks on top of the ground.

The sky splits up when a tornado is there,
Things around start to tear.
In this darkness many go mad,
Leaving some families very sad.

Darkness spills over the sky,
At this sight, many will cry.
Swirling, swishing faster than light,
The tornado thunders throughout the night.

Rohan Kataria (11)
Reddiford School

FRIENDS FOREVER
(For all my mates at Reddiford and Sacred Heart School)

Although it's quite a statement
Well it happens to be true
The best friend I've ever had
I'm glad to say is you.

You're there if I should need you
And you never turn away
I know that I can count on you
24 hours a day.

We've had our problems
As nearly everybody does
But arguments never last that long
With special mates like us.

Some people have so many mates
With whom they spend their time
But no one has a special mate
As fabulous as mine.

So thank you for always being there
Your friendship's strong and true
And I just want to let you know
I'm always there for you.

Through sun, rain, light and dark
24 hours a day
I always want to hear you say
'Friends forever, you and I, people can always see.'

Katie Walsh (10)
Reddiford School

WINTER

The crisp winter's sky
Darkens earlier than ever,
The cold mist begins to grow
Over the cold land.
The snow begins to fall
Covering the world with a blanket.

The children play with the delicate snow,
The snowflakes falling in a perfect pattern
Dropping swiftly like a swallow from the frozen sky.
The roads - nothing but the soft, crunchy snow
Waiting for the children's gentle touch
As they build their beautiful snowmen.

Welcome Snow Queen from the heavens above,
With ice-piercing blue eyes
Watching over the amazing fragile snow.
The winter cries for her awesome wisdom.
For winter would be lost if it wasn't for her magical touch
As she dazzles the children with her magic.

Christmas comes with a wonderful setting,
The presents are shared and children thank Santa Claus.
Families gather for their delicious dinners,
Crackers are popped, choirs sing.
But sadly winter says goodbye,
But arrives back next year after the cold January and February.

Jamie Russell (10)
Reddiford School

DISCO DIVA!

Her dreaming eye sees the glory
Flashing her life as a fairy story
Her name amidst the stars
People come from near and far.

To the cheers of old and young
The hands that swirl and twirl
Passion speaking under sparkling lights
Slender sprite makes a dazzling sight.

Sweat and tears
Facing nameless fears
Hard work and skill
She longed for that special thrill.

And now she stands so proud
Tears of happiness in the crowd
Disco Diva is her name
Finally she has her day of fame.

Anoushka Mehta (10)
Reddiford School

UNDER THE SEA

Under the sea
What can there be?

Riches or gold or hidden treasures.

Under the sea
What will we see?

A world with such different pleasures.

Under the sea
What will there be?

Fishes, whales and colourful seaweed.

Under the sea
What can we see?

A world that is magic, with no greed.

Aileda Mortimer (11)
Reddiford School

AN ODE TO BESS

Oh my sweetheart
Bess the name
When I look at your juicy red lips
How I dream to kiss them
I've never had a prize so good
I do not wish to share
When I whistle a tune at your window
I admire you plaiting a dark red love knot in your black silky hair
Those jet-black eyes stare at me
How I love your perfume
I cherish you
I worship you
You're everything to me
Wait for me by moonlight
Watch for me by moonlight
I'll be there
Waiting for a kiss from you my angel.

Misha Mansigani (10)
Reddiford School

AN AIR RAID

Would they come again tonight?
Surely not, it was Sabbath night.
Twenty-seven nights in a row,
Of buildings collapsing and fires aglow.

Off went that sound again,
That deafening, screeching siren.
I was out of my bed, as quick as a flash,
Grabbed gas mask, torch and a little cash.

I came out of the house and looked around,
Followed the crowd towards that staircase, leading down,
Looking up into the sky, while stretching and yawning,
Would all the buildings be there in the morning?

Down underground they were short of spaces,
I looked around and saw all the familiar faces.
I found myself a bed and tucked myself tight,
and settled in for a very long night.

Suddenly I woke up to the sound of a shatter,
Was that my house that went down with a clatter?
I could not sleep with all the loud noise,
So I sat up and played with my aeroplane toys.

My brother would be up there right now,
Spitfires versus Heinkels and Stukas, wow!
My dad was in Stalag 8b, he never laughs,
And Mum would be working with the other WAAFS.

After a while, although it seemed like a year,
The bombing had stopped, and off went the all-clear.
The baker's and butcher's, that had been there before,
Were now only rubble lying on the floor.
Then I glanced at my own little home,
It was still standing, but all on its own.

Tom Farmer (11)
Reddiford School

MY BEST FRIEND

My best friend is early in the morning
Always ready never yawning
He's got good footwear, works hard all day
I need his advice; I wonder what he'll say
He's a TV I need to stare
A friend like him is very rare
He's custard, very exquisite
I think he needs to come and visit
He's an action figure, very cool
I think he follows every rule
Always to good things there are some bad
Occasionally he would get a little mad
He's a tiger, as brave as they come
No one would ever dare call him dumb
Every month or two he would go to Italy
Each time visiting the town of Scilly
Alas one day he did not come home
He went to stay in beautiful Rome.

Vedaant Patel (11)
Reddiford School

WATER IS WONDERFUL

Water, water everywhere
Rushing past
Without a care.

Water keeps us alive
Falling down
From the skies
It keeps us living
It keeps us ticking.

Water, water everywhere
Rushing past
Without a care.

Cleaning knives
And washing clothes
Water sometimes
Heals your bones
It's there for you
When you can swim
It's always good in your skin.

Water, water everywhere
Rushing past
Without a care.

In your baths
And in your showers
Cleaning you
And cleaning me
We appear clean
As can be.

Water, water everywhere
Rushing past
Without a care.

Jason Ting (11)
Reddiford School

A WICKED CURSE

The mysterious gaze of the gleaming green eyes
of an ebony-coated cat makes me tense with fear
and I suddenly shiver in the tranquil, chilly, moonlit night.

I experience queer happenings during the night
like the strange howling of the wind, witches zooming
and flying on their broomsticks, casting evil curses
and spells upon me.

The wicked screams and laughter of the witches haunt me
throughout the day.
The bubbling of their magical potions makes my stomach turn.

I am nasty to my friends, I push and shove, I shout and scream at them.
I answer back to my teachers and break all the rules.
I don't say please or thank you.

I've been cursed.

Serena Mehta (8)
Reddiford School

MY BROTHER

My brother is sometimes as kind as a kitten
He is also an annoying wasp, always buzzing around me
My brother sometimes hurts me, the stings are very painful
He is a hard wooden chair and a rainy day
My brother is a blue-purple colour
But he is a pizza with different toppings at various times of day
I do not know what to expect.

My brother is scruffy footwear
He is a maze, always getting lost
He is a talking robot
My brother is a tall, slim tree trunk in its firm roots
He is Spain because he is dramatic.

Krupa Patel (10)
Reddiford School

BOMBS

As the bombs rained down on us
We ran to the little air raid shed
We closed the door and listened
I could hear the Hawker Hurricane circling above
About to drop a bomb on us
Instead of hearing a bomb drop down
We heard a series of rapid gunshots
Which I thought came from a machine gun.
The next moment we heard a tremendous crash
As an aircraft crashed down on the ground
And the enemy pilot was gone for good.

Krishna Patel (10)
Reddiford School

SPRING ARRIVES

As spring comes and the church bells ring
The daffodil buds uncurl
The gorgeous pink blossoms cover the trees
Swaying beneath the captivating sunlight
As it winks away
Roses wine-red prickling my posterior as I meander by
Lilies, the hue of the sun scenting the breeze
As they spin around having fun
Orange blossoms seen at a distance
Lurching in the spring flurry.

Fluttering birds humming a melodious tune in the bright blue sky
Spring so beautiful making hearts dance and sing
Welcoming joyously the finest time of the year.

This is the way to give glory to the rest of the golden world
Then I will say words of sincerity
Oh! What a happy time of the year
To enjoy this sensation of living after as hankering anticipation.

Neha Shukla (9)
Reddiford School

MY ODE TO A CHOCOLATE BUTTON!

Your creamy, sweet white chocolate taste melts in my mouth instantly.
Your divine unique taste makes me dribble on my clothes.
Your friendliness entertains me, especially at snack time.
I adore your family, the milk chocolate ones especially.
They are so exquisite, like you!
Your delectable taste fills my little tummy promptly.
Your titillating taste flatters my taste buds immediately.
I will not eat any other chocolate nor will I wear any other button
As you're simply the best by far!

Devika Devani (10)
Reddiford School

THE SEASIDE

The sea is blue,
The sea is green,
The waves flow
Like a mesmerising dream.

The sand is soft,
Grains small as pins,
The sand grabs out,
My feet sink in.

As ice creams are bought
People look at attractions,
The donkey ride's great
And that's just a fraction.

The sea is full
Of many a dish,
Out come the rods
And fish, fish, fish.

When everyone's gone home,
The sea life stops to listen,
The noise is no more
And the seaside glistens.

Benjamin Hallam (10)
Reddiford School

FLOWERS

Poppies, tulips, pansies, roses
All different aromas, sizes and shapes
Petals like colours of butterflies' wings
You stand with a delicate sunrise pose
Your petals hang with morning dew
Hang on you like a halo golden ring.

In spring the flower buds burst
The daily workers, butterflies and bees
They come and go with never a wink
You make people happy whatever the weather
And stand with pride until winter arrives.

Michelle Lam (9)
Reddiford School

THE CENTRE OF MY LIFE

The warmth of the room could brighten up anybody
It is the centre of my life
The walls are decorated with bright warming patterns
It is my protected fort where I can seek refuge from the rattling
noise of reality
The walls are covered in posters as the bed fits comfortably
into a small corner
The shelves are crammed with wonderful books ranging from the
good old days of Treasure Island to the horrible days of the holocaust
It is a place where I can soothe away the worries of this hectic lifestyle
It is a place where I can escape from the harsh reality and enter
a new world of my own
It is a room full of wonders yet an asylum of boredom

The centre of the room is my beautiful bed
The soft, warm duvet is the centre of comfort while the pillow is
as soft as the wool from a sheep
It is a place where my imagination can run wild and I can dream
of a world of my own
A world where anything is possible
A world where I can see what I want to see and there's nobody
to boss you around.

Muhammed Gulamhusein (10)
Reddiford School

THE DARK LIFE OF THE CHIMNEY SWEEP

He woke in the dark
He worked in the dark
He trapped in the dark
The dark cage that eludes all
The dark cage that conceals all
The dark of life!
Death is but a doorway
Death takes us from the pain
The horror
And the misery
And unites us with our Lord
But before this happens
We must fulfil our duty
To a chimney sweep
This a pain ridden way
A destructive
Torturous way

The fire was beneath him
The rats above him
Clambering up crying
With the brush in his hand
He fell!
He fell to the glory
He fell to the kingdom
He fell to death!

Varun Anand (10)
Reddiford School

DOWN AT THE BOTTOM OF THE DEEP BLUE SEA

Down at the bottom of the deep blue sea
where the sacred sharks swim after me

Down at the bottom of the deep blue sea
where all the special starfish stick to me

Down at the bottom of the deep blue sea
where there is still hidden, gleaming gold

Down at the bottom of the deep blue sea
where there are still some stories to be told.

George Corrigan (11)
Reddiford School

COLOURS OF SPRING

Now that it has stopped snowing
And the wind has stopped blowing
Everything starts growing.

The whole world turns green
The freshest colour I've ever seen
After the dull dark winter scene.

I try very hard and think
I close my eyes and blink
Suddenly the world has turned blossom pink.

Now the yellow sun is bright
The world is full of light
Spring is a beautiful sight.

Deniz Baris (9)
Reddiford School

MALDINI'S TALE

It was Milan vs. Inter,
Shevchenko vs. Pinter,
The players were cold, it was winter,
Milan were going to beat Inter.

First attempt, Albertini's cross,
Got to Ronaldo, but made a loss,
The goal posts were lonely, they're gathering moss,
The Inter manager was very cross.

Second attempt, Seedorf's shot,
Bound to go in, Abbiati stops,
Vieri goes in, what a pop!
Didn't score but made an excellent shot.

Last minute Maldini shoots!
What a classic, breaks his boots!
The crowd were getting ready to loot,
Milan won thanks to Maldini's boots!

The manager was awarded with a glimmering crown,
The Inter players put on a big frown,
Maldini was gifted a million pounds,
His colleagues passed him the glimmering crown.

The next day he was followed by a hoarding crowd,
Not only were they big but they were extremely loud,
Maldini ran away, he was totally cowed,
But he couldn't escape he hoarding crowd.

He had interviews and was asked how he felt,
'I have so many fans,' he said, his heart started to melt,
He started to scramble away from the cameras, he thought enough
damage was dealt,
Now he knew how David Beckham felt.

Sanam Shah (11)
Reddiford School

Tiger

Enemies beware!

You won't know what's hit you
As he sets upon you

He is the largest of the cats
With camouflage skin
Makes you wonder what you could be looking at

His eyes are like dark, piercing pins
Which catch every moving victim

His paws with five silhouette nails
Are just like a jagged knife

His sharp, dazzling white teeth
With which he can tear through anything
Are just like sharp shining blades

But friends, don't be afraid

Caress the comfy, thick, fur coat
And you will feel like you're in Heaven

Have his black and white striped tail
Around your neck as well
It would send you to sleep in great comfort

And should he lie on his back
It would just look like a simple layer of pure white snow.

Ahsan Jamil (8)
Reddiford School

THE MATCH OF THE YEAR - ARSENAL VS MAN UTD

The FA Cup Final, the match of the year,
Thousands were watching with glasses of beer.
They came out the tunnel and into the light,
The screams from the fans gave them a fright.

The ref blew the whistle, the game moved on,
The cup would decide whoever had won.
The first half was boring right up to the end,
But just before the whistle a holy wish was sent.

Giggs took the ball and ran down the wing,
He got in a cross and Beckham had a swing.
The ball hit the post and came out to Scholes,
Back of the net - one of the best goals.

Kick-off second half - pretty much the same,
Very, very boring, like the whole game.
Until along came a spark, a glimmer of hope,
A draw for Arsenal was looking in scope.

Pires took a shot from about halfway,
The ball hit the crossbar, came back in play.
It came out to Henry, he took a shot,
Goal for Arsenal to even the plot.

It went into penalties - extra time did nothing,
There were no more chances to run up the wing.
It was all up to them - this one for the crown,
Conquer this, and no need for a frown.

The first eight went in, but the last two were tense,
Pires knew he would score, he had some fore sense.
Pires had scored! It was all up to Keane,
If he missed this everyone would be mean.

He ran up to take it, he was looking to score,
Seaman had to save it, he'd get the cup and much more.
Well done to the Gunners, well done Arsenal,
And a special thanks to Seaman for saving us all.

Alex Parker (11)
Reddiford School

THE BUGATTI VEYRON

The Bugatti Veyron is the fastest car ever made
It is so fast that no one could ever pay
It has a top speed of two hundred and fifty-two miles per hour
And nine hundred and eighty-seven brake horse power
It cost six hundred and forty thousand pounds
And it makes an incredible amount of sound
It has gigantic wheels and posh interior
At raised position a spoiler at the rear
It has an 8.3 litre V12 engine
And it does not need any kind of mending
It has leather lined seats and a small gear stick
And the steering wheel that definitely isn't a trick.

The speedometer reads to two hundred and eighty miles per hour
It is so big, it has so much raw power
It has four small turbo chargers that increase the speed of the car
You'll be able to go to France and back because it can go far
As I get older I dream of owning this car
To sit behind the wheel and travel afar
The purr of its engine as the key ignites
The burn of the rubber is up for a fight
I pushed down the handbrake, pulled up the clutch
The intensity rises as I feel the adrenaline rush.

Shiv Mistry (10)
Reddiford School

THE DARKNESS AND THE MOON

The moon swept across the sky and will never die
The bright shining moon swept across the sky and will never die
The darkness soon came and swept the lightness away
The river was still as concrete
A boat spoilt my reflection
And floated up the sand
And thy man in the boat came up to me and said
'You are thy one, you are my son.'

Vishal Patel (10)
Reddiford School

MY BEYBLADE

I love my fantastic Beyblade
Which spins round and round.
It is a light blue turquoise shade
Which also makes a wheezing and whirring sound.

Some are big,
Some are small,
Some can break a twig
Or even light up the hall.

Some of them fight,
Some of them glow
Which is a wonderful sight
Or even a spectacular show.

I just adore my Beyblades!

Rushil Malde (9)
Reddiford School

MY FRIEND!

Her golden hair blows in the wind, so soft and silky
Her chestnut darting eyes spot me from afar
The twinkle in them signals a kind, cheerful person
She's a soft fluffy poodle, sweet and cuddly
She always has a huge grin on her face
I know when she's coming as her sweet aroma drifts towards me
She cheers me up when I'm sad and makes everyone laugh
Sometimes our friendship falls apart like a jigsaw
but the pieces are found again!
We'll always be friends and that's guaranteed!

Meera Bharania (11)
Reddiford School

LOVE

The sweet kiss of a baby trying to make me feel better
The loving scent of happy roses.

My Valentine card has lots of love in it
Love is everything you can imagine.

The soul of people's love is in my heart
My heart is full of loving care.

Love is the true word of God
If you have love you are a hero.

I will have love till the end
Love is what you must have!

Jeevan Dhillon (8)
Reddiford School

WINTER

Now the summer has gone,
As it was the last seconds as the sun shone.
The clouds and the wind had to come,
When it was time to snow and have fun.

People tried to keep cosy in their houses,
The rats snuggled with the mouses.
As the air outside started to chill,
When you no longer could see the top of the hill.

Snowflakes fell gently on the ground,
Some were big, some were round.
It covered the street and the hound
And nothing later was to be found.

As I came out to have fun and play,
I'd wished the snow would still stay.
There were lots of activities, snowballing and snowman building,
This was a snowy scene for me!

Bengi Yildirimoglu (11)
Reddiford School

THE LINE OF LIFE

Life is a wobbly line,
It's a rich deep scarlet wine.
It twists and turns,
Has ups and downs.
It has its smiles
And it has its frowns.
This is a line that you cannot cut,
It ends . . . abrupt.

Ravi Vekaria (10)
Reddiford School

IF I COULD RULE THE WORLD

As a ruler of the world . . .
I would help all the poor
I would give them food and shelter
And would give them so much more.

As a ruler of the world . . .
I would stop all the wars,
By helping people listen and talk
And make them obey the laws.

As a ruler of the world . . .
I would decree,
To help endangered tigers, elephants
And all the fish in the sea.

As a ruler of the world . . .
I would rule with kindness
And teach to be tolerant,
My world would be filled with happiness.

Shamir Vekaria (9)
Reddiford School

HAPPINESS

H   appiness is my way of life
A   las it rebukes me from feeling blue
P   lease stand up if you are joyful
P   lease stand up and celebrate
I   love the tingling feeling
N   ot the unhappy one
E   njoyment is my way of life
S   o come on be like me
S   o come and rejoice with me.

Subomi Anidugbe (10)
Reddiford School

WINTER

Winter is a dull time when everyone is cold
There are no leaves on the trees
Lots of woolly hats are sold

Everyone is tucked up inside their cosy beds
We all have to make sure that all the animals are fed

The ice is at freezing point
The ducks can now not swim
Watch out skaters
You might just break a limb

All the roads are blocked
The gritters have not been
Hurry, hurry, hurry
They're nowhere to be seen

Snowballs are thrown, thrown, thrown
Snowballs are thrown
It's really a lot of fun

On the 25th of December
Presents are given and shared
Lots and lots of chocolate
To be shared with family and friends

An extra layer is needed
Just to make sure
You won't get any frostbite
They can get really sore

In a cold winter
When all the birds had fled
Someone made a snowman
And put a woolly hat on his head

Winter is a dull time when everyone is cold
But still enjoy your winters, before you grow too old!

Helen Farmer (10)
Reddiford School

COLOURS

Colour, colour everywhere,
Makes you stand,
Makes you stare.

Salty sea water is the colour of blue,
It's also the colour of morning dew.

Green is the colour of emerald trees,
Yellow is the colour of chunky cheese.

Red is the colour of viscous blood,
Brown is the colour of runny mud.

Purple for the pansy's lazy head,
Just getting ready to go to bed.

Gold for my precious football medal,
Silver is the colour of my bicycle pedal.

Colour, colour everywhere,
Makes you stand,
Makes you stare.

Lawrence Xu (9)
Reddiford School

MY GARDEN

My garden is a portal through space and time
Where fairies shimmer, glimmer and dance
Underneath the old oak tree
Lives a family of three.

One sits beneath the leaves
And stares and reads
One snoozes in a patch of daisies
Never opening a droopy eye
One frolics in the autumn breeze
And slithers in the summer seas.

And the bees buzzing frequently in the hot sun
A fleet of butterflies flutter their rainbow-coloured wings
This is my garden of magical things!

Priya Abrol (10)
Reddiford School

THE SUN

An orange and yellow tennis ball,
Trapped on a blue and white piece of card,
With strong rays of light as a torch with new batteries.

Brings a ray of happy faces,
He smiles from the sky,
Chuckling as we get a brown or red tan from his vigorous light.

He stays until night then swaps duties with the moon,
The sky changes colour as we all wave goodbye,
And the moon takes her place shimmering
And watching over us all until dawn.

Catherine Tanna (10)
Reddiford School

A Castle

I want to live in a castle with bowmen everywhere,
Shooting down the enemies, who brandish silverware.
I want to live in a castle with mountains everywhere
And when I look around me, wildlife blocks my glare.

I'd like to live in a castle 'cause I'd be in charge of it all
And I would have lots of servants at my disposal.
I'd like to live in a castle with winding spiral stairs
And whenever I'd get down them I would tell everyone there.

And if a nasty dragon came terribly close to me,
I'd strap on all my armour and chase it away with my spear.
But then again it depends, if I'll ever be next for the throne,
'Cause my dad isn't a king and I live in an ordinary home.

Dominic Keen (10)
Reddiford School

Memories

Here lies the body of Solaman Peas
Under the daisies, under the trees.
Peas aren't here, only the pod
Peas shelled out and went home to God.

Over the Earth into space,
Went the astronauts with courage and faith.
Off went the rocket into the unknown
Not knowing whether they'll return home.

Now going into happiness
Trying to find love,
Here comes Valentine's Day
With red roses and cards.

Serena Patel (9)
Reddiford School

THE BEACH

The pleasant sea gently swaying
The small children running around and playing
The sun-kissed people sitting down
The bright white seagulls flapping around
The crystal-clear water making no sound
The gentle wind slowly blowing on the beach
A poor red frisbee tossed into the sea now sadly out of reach
The driftwood lying on the corn coloured sand
The bright coloured instruments played by the band
A little boat going by
The sun began to say goodbye
The beautiful sunset in the sky

The rough swishing from side to side
No little children anywhere
The cold icy wind blowing across the beach
One old man with his dog going for a walk
The only soul with no one to talk to
The sad seagull frantically searching for scrap
The dark grey waters showing their horrid worse
The gloomy sky covers the sun like a dark sheet over a light
The bare beach hopelessly waiting for summer
The faint sun goes down early
The abandoned beach waits to see another bright, joyful summer.

Akash Alexander (10)
Reddiford School

COLOUR

There is a colourful rainbow in the sky
With arches that are as blue as the clear deep sea
And as yellow as the bright golden sun
And like a marigold and black buzzing bee.

There is an orange sunset beautiful and soft
On the trees there are lots of emerald juicy pears
Stars sparkle like shiny white diamonds in the sky
In the forest we see brown huge fierce bears.

Afzal Roked (8)
Reddiford School

I SAW A JOLLY SAILOR

(Based on 'I Saw A Jolly Hunter' by Charles Causley)

I saw a jolly sailor
Sailing on the sea
Steered the boat right
Then looking at me!

Sailed to jolly land
Walking on his feet
Saw jolly shop
To buy jolly sweet!

Shopkeeper jolly criminal
Was very bad
Stole jolly boat
Now sailor jolly mad!

Sailor jolly police
Went to jolly port
Got into search plane
Shopkeeper in a fort!

Police jolly shopkeeper
Put in jolly jail
Sad shopkeeper
No jolly mail!

Akshay Baldota (9)
Reddiford School

GOODBYE GYMNASTICS

My cartwheels are terrible
I cannot do them right
My somersaults are messy
My joints are too tight

Standing on my head
I keep falling to the ground
It feels like I'm sitting
On the merry-go-round

Walking on a beam
Gives me dizzy spells
In my head go ringing
Thousands of bells

My balance is awful
I do not have a hope
How on earth will I
Ever walk on a rope

My rollovers are hopeless
And splits are pretty bad
And when this year is over
I will be very glad

I'll move over now
Leave gymnastics alone
Next year I'm getting
Into computer zone!

Alysha Bhatti (8)
Reddiford School

SUMMER GOES

Summer goes, summer goes
Like the sand between my toes
Leaves me standing today
When the waves go out
That's how summer pulls away
Waiting for the school bus.

Summer brought, summer brought
All the frogs that I have caught
Fogging in the pond
Hot dogs, flowers, shells and rocks
Postcards in my postcard box
With joyful messages.

Summer took, summer took
All the lessons in my book
Blew them far away
I forgot the things that I knew
Arithmetic and spelling too.

Summer's gone, summer's gone
Fall and winter coming on
Frost in the morning
Makes me cold
Nothing else is quite that bad
Only slip in the rain.

Kishan Patel (9)
Reddiford School

THE YOUNG MAN IN A RACE

His pale blue eyes fade in the sun
His good appearance too
As we all see him run
In his multicoloured shoes.

His hairy arms
Pass through the air
But only the audience it charms
Because the others do not think it is fair.

The sun beams down harder on his face
So one of the runners calls it a day
But the young man keeps up the pace
And makes the other runners pay.

The young man won the race
And had victory with the cup
Because the other runners
Could not keep up the pace.

Jamie Sadheura (10)
Reddiford School

SPRINGTIME

Spring is here
It is my favourite time of the year
The wind is blowing
And flowers are growing

The children are playing
The grass is swaying
The sun is shining
Everyone is smiling

Lots of people are having fun
Under the blazing sun
The scent of flowers
Is overpowering

The birds are calling
Winter leaves are falling
Spring is here
And it is my favourite time of the year.

Akash Sharma (9)
Reddiford School

FLOWER POWER

Oh dear flower
how powerful you are.

Your bright coloured petals
make me feel cheerful and alive.

You bring life to my garden
to make it a better place to play and relax.

Your scent is as fragrant
as my mother's sweet perfume.

You made my grandmother glow
when she was feeling blue.

Your leaf even cured my hand
when I was stung by a stinging nettle.

You provide food for the birds and the bees
as they help to spread your glorious beauty round the world.

Oh dear flower
how powerful and beautiful you are.

Venetia Patel (9)
Reddiford School

My Christmas Stocking
(Based on 'Magic Box' by Kit Wright)

I will put in my Christmas stocking . . .
The echoing and deafening Santa's ho, ho, ho!
A ring carved from crystal ice
Bright glow of Rudolph's red nose, like a cherry
A halo made out of glistening white snow.

I will put in my Christmas stocking . . .
The magnificent and endless signature of Santa's
A sweet voice from angel Gabriel
The speechless loud laughing of an excited boy
A shining old ruby from Herald's crown.

I will put in my Christmas stocking . . .
The ear-splitting sounds of crackers going snap!
The infinite, number of Santa's footprints in the snow
The sparkling faces of sweet angels
My wonderful dreams of the three presents I really want.

I will put in my Christmas stocking . . .
The sparkling swish of a fairy waving her magical wand
The bright shining gold of ringing bells
The dazzling lights from a decorated Christmas tree
An eternal prayer for all the poor and homeless children.

Rikhil Shah (8)
Reddiford School

Ode To The Highwayman

Hail, o' highwayman,
How I love thee,
So bold you are and bravely you ride,
With your pistol butts a-twinkle,
Your rapier hilt sparkling in the moonlight,

Your eyes glittering under the stars,
As you kissed my rippling hair in the moonlight,
O' how I treasure that moment,
You shall be back and I'll be waiting,
Plaiting a dark red love knot into my long black hair.

Victoria Pearson (10)
Reddiford School

ONION LOVE

Not at all a satin kiss or a sweet smelling rose
This Valentine's Day darling, I shall give you an onion
It is a magical moon wrapped in brown carbon paper
It promises colourful light
Like the wonderful growth of love.

Taste it
Its fierce kiss will unite our lips
Possessive and faithful until the end
When you go I shall come too, for I would not be able to bear the pain.

Take it
Its platinum loops will shrink to a wedding ring if you wish
Lethal
Its scent will cling to your fingers
Cling to your knife.

I am always dreaming of you with that golden onion
Every Valentine's Day our love for each other seems to get bigger
                                                    and bigger.

Whoever thought an onion was that special.

Meera Relwani (9)
Reddiford School

FIREWORKS

Fireworks are giant explosives
That go up into the refreshing air
And fall down like crocodile tears

Some are like never-ending spinning wheels
When they bang I feel like my heart has stopped beating
Their shapes are very strange and round

They are as colourful as a rainbow and peacock feathers
They remind me of a midnight feast
Some are the size of a pine tree.

Amish Mehta (8)
Reddiford School

FIREWORKS

Have you seen magic in the sky
In the fireworks' display at night?
They rise and colour the deep blue sky
Like fountains of flame and stars.

All colours bright and gay -
Crimson, green, blue, orangy spray,
The Catherine wheels begin to whirl
Like speedy yo-yos which twirl.

It's fun for the children, fun for all,
Happiness and joy to share with all,
It comes every year with new delight
To greet everybody the festival of light.

Ayesha Dasgupta (9)
Reddiford School

MICE

I think mice
Are rather nice

> Their tails are long
> Their faces small
> They haven't any chins at all
> Their ears are pink
> Their teeth are white
> They run about
> The house at night
> They nibble things
> They shouldn't touch
> And no one seems
> To like them much

But I think mice
Are nice.

Priya Patel
Reddiford School

ORANGE

The orange is as bright as the sun
It reminds me of a squeaky toy
The shape is like a round ball
It makes me feel juicy inside
It gives me all the vitamins I need
It's got tiny seeds with bitter taste
It gives me all of the strength that I can get
It makes me feel happy, that's why I want to eat it.

Jasminder Sagoo (9)
Reddiford School

MONTHS - HAIKUS

Cold January
In the middle of winter
Waiting for summer

It's the month for love
The month to show your feelings
To other people

September is here
It's near the end of summer
We are starting school

November's arrived
Guy Fawkes is due to happen
On our Bonfire Night

It's now December
Christmas is now beginning
And the new year starts.

Sasha Chandar-Seale (11)
Ryefield Primary School

QUESTION AND ANSWER POEM

Where do we go after life?
To the land of forever
How do stars glow?
With the smiles of the world
How do birds fly?
On the breath of God
When will the sun die?
When love is extinct.

Josh Whitfield (10)
Ryefield Primary School

WHY?

What is the moon?
The reflecting light of the world.
Who is God?
A figure of light that will stick in our minds for eternity.
Why does a tree sway?
To keep up with the windy moans of time.
What is a bird?
A flying, swooping animal that flutters by my window.
What is water?
The splashing memories of our childhoods.
Why do we die?
So God can praise us with eternal life.

Zoë Whelehan (11)
Ryefield Primary School

A GOLDEN STAR

I see a star tonight
A star golden and bright
I see it up above
I think it's filled with love
A star so bright
I can't believe its light
It twinkles in the sky
Way, way up high
Standing on its own
Looking all alone
Its golden reflection shines
I wish it could be mine.

Tierney Harris (11)
Ryefield Primary School

ANIMALS

Big-gobber
Fish-catcher
High-jumper
Loud-screecher
Tail-walker
Good-trainer
Shark-dodger

Tail-wagler
Loud-barker
Good-sniffer
Good-trainer
Very-furry
Loadsa-energy
Very-smelly

Good-hider
Tiny-animals
Big-animals
Multi-coloured
Big-eater
Water-skier.

Lacey Smith (10)
Ryefield Primary School

SNOW

Snow is white and bright
And it comes down silently
Children having fun
Making snowballs and snowmen
Wishing it would come again.

Shorifa Khatun (10)
Ryefield Primary School

QUESTION AND ANSWER POEM

Where does life begin?
When you first breathe.

What is light?
Stronger than dark.

Why is the sea blue?
Because it is God's favourite colour.

Why is the grass greener on the other side?
Because there is a dark side and a light side.

Why is everything about money?
Because more people like it.

Why is everything coloured?
Because God didn't like the colour grey.

Natalie Munday (10)
Ryefield Primary School

QUESTION AND ANSWER POEM

When will there be no life?
When the last blade of grass turns brown.
When will the sun be put out?
When it burns out its wick.
When will we be able to turn back time?
When we can make every clock tick backwards.
When will there be no books?
When the last person dislikes reading.
When will there be no Milky Way?
When the last star loses its shine.

Jack Taylor (10)
Ryefield Primary School

KING OF THE STARS

He comes out with the stars,
His face is glowing,
His skin is smooth and his eyes are bright,
His hair is ruffled,
He wears pyjamas, decorated with stars,
His lips sparkle in the moonlight,
His teeth are studded with blue diamonds.

He is a kind gentleman,
He will comfort you with his stars,
He keeps you safe,
He makes you think of sweet dreams,
He is a loving grandpa, with a big heart.

He lives among the stars,
He watches you,
His blue diamond eyes look down on you,
He moves swiftly among the stars,
He tiptoes around the world,
He is safe
And looks after me while I sleep.

Georgia Bowers (11)
Ryefield Primary School

BAXTER THE DOG

Standing motionless
His eyes transfixed on his ball
Anticipation
Head tilting hearing each word
His wagging tail cuts the air.

Simon Brown (10)
Ryefield Primary School

HAIKU CALENDAR

Summer afternoon
Let's go in the swimming pool
Where is my costume?

In spring flowers grow
I love the pinkie blossoms
My mum waters them.

Autumn leaves falling
We must sweep all the leaves up
The broom snapped in half.

Winter snow falling
Get out your winter sledge now
I will pull you fast.

Megan Horwood (11)
Ryefield Primary School

WHAT TEACHERS DO

Fast-thinker
Coffee-drinker

Brain-tickler
Work-giver

Book-marker
Home-worker

Sometimes-shouting
Never-doubting.

Michael Purvey (11)
Ryefield Primary School

AT THE END OF THE DAY WHEN HE COMES OUT

At the end of the day
When he comes out
The moon shines brightly
With the light so misty.

I stay up to watch him
Moving from house to house
So swiftly he moves
No sound yet very quickly.

The lovely smile when he meets me
He greets me with his special charm
Not a word he says when he fills me with happiness
But soon he disappears.

Out of the lake those dark colours
They appear with his face full of glee
He draws pictures with stars
The stars fill his eyes so bright.

His name is Sir Night
Out of the bushes comes his friend
While he disappears to
The other end of Earth.

This mysterious man
So swiftly he moves
I will soon see him again
At the end of the day.

Nicola Fish (11)
Ryefield Primary School

QUESTION AND ANSWER POEM

Where does life begin?
As our eyes begin to open
Why were we born?
To see our future
How do we live?
Like a silent turtle going by
When does our life begin?
When you are in the real world
How do we move?
With our sense of humour we produce
When does life end?
When we close our eyes and never awake.

Georgia Carroll (11)
Ryefield Primary School

DOWN TO EARTH

When will the sea rise?
When God's last groan was made.
What is a newborn child?
A gorgeous and beautiful baby.
What is thunder?
The everlasting groan of God.
What are friends?
The ones you will love and cherish forever.
Who is God?
The merciful and glorious person on Earth.
What is school?
For education and ability.

Hajjar Mouak (10)
Ryefield Primary School

AGE-MAKER

Lettuce-eater   Thumb-walker

    Body-shelter

Slow-mover   Ground-walker

    Sleepy-player

Age-maker   Slow-muncher.

Jodie Newell (10)
Ryefield Primary School

BEING ALONE

Depressed sad people
They grow older with no friends
Anxious for some love
Wandering the streets alone
Fighting their lives for love.

Simone Downie (10)
Ryefield Primary School

MY LOVED HAMSTER

Sleeping in the day
Scampering about at night
Climbing up the cage
In its ball on the ground floor
We will find him safe and sound.

Georgina Pym (11)
Ryefield Primary School

THE NIGHT

With no family
Breathing heavily
Alone, frightened, scared
Unknown shadows haunting me
Heartless as I sleep dreamless.

Tom Green (11)
Ryefield Primary School

MY PRINCIPAL

My principal smells of old socks
My principal looks like a alien from outer space
My principal wears the same clothes every day
So I think he wears the same pants too
He makes me feel sick when I walk past him
So beware, cause I think all principals are evil.

Molly Scarff (9)
St Christopher's Preparatory School, Wembley

SILENT SILENCE

Silence is more silent
Than the paddling of cats' paws
Silence is more silent
Than trees rustling
Silence is more silent
Than the waves splashing
But the noisiest sound
Is you shouting.

Jack Talboys (9)
St Christopher's Preparatory School, Wembley

SNOW DAY

'Can I have a snow fight?'
'No, you'll get snow on you.'
'But it's only snow.'
'It'll come off, then when you come inside you'll leave trails of snow.'
'Oh yes, I forgot about that. Can I make a snowman?'
'No! Now be quiet you're driving me crazy!'
'Can I make a snow slide?'
'No! And you're grounded for two weeks!'
'Why?'
'Because you're driving me up the wall!'

John Okunpolor (9)
St Christopher's Preparatory School, Wembley

SENSES

I feel like a criminal . . .
I hear trees rustling through the window
I smell damp corners
I taste bitter food when I eat it
I see dark walls wherever I look
    Where am I?

I feel anguished by the torture . . .
I hear people screaming with pain and agony
I smell awful because of no baths
I taste nothing because the food they give me ruins my taste buds
I see dark corners everywhere except through the window.
    Where am I?
    You decide.

Raees Lunat (8)
St Christopher's Preparatory School, Wembley

KENYA

Cattle in the fields
Sometimes dirty water
Nomads walking around
Waiting for friends to get ready for journeys
Little girls and boys striding to school
Sharing desks among three
Do you?
Mums and dads working in fields picking snow peas
Dads feeding the cows and calves
Not me
Where do we live?
We live in hot Kenya
But don't forget
It is quite dangerous.

Aanvika Amin (9)
St Christopher's Preparatory School, Wembley

IN THE WOOD

I'm alone in the wood
With the tall, tall treetops rustling behind me
The sky is pitch-black
With the wind whistling around me
I see rats running everywhere

Slimy, slithery snakes
Sliding everywhere
I hear hooting from an owl from a distance
The grass is grey and I see a black cat walking beside me
It was dark
Very dark indeed.

Mark Paszkowski (8)
St Christopher's Preparatory School, Wembley

THE OLD MAN

Every day the old man
Sits in his deckchair
Staring and staring
But who is he staring at?
Nobody knows but
The old man

Every day the old man
Sits in his deckchair
Whistling and whistling
And what is he whistling?
Nobody knows but
The old man

Now I know the truth
He was staring at you
Not me but you
And what was he whistling?
Nobody knows but
The old man.

Katy Sacks (9)
St Christopher's Preparatory School, Wembley

TEASED

Every day I get teased
Just because I am small
In my inner thoughts I think I am tall
Every day I hold my tears and my heart sinks down
Like throwing a stone into the river
I feel lonely at school because that is where I get teased
Nobody knows at school
Nobody cares at school.

Regina Sabaratnam (8)
St Christopher's Preparatory School, Wembley

WOOD

I'm very scared alone in the wood
Where the grass is grey
And the trees over black
And the wind is whistling behind me
I'm seeing rats and cats in front of me
I hear whistling, rustling, hooting and hissing
I'm scared
Very scared indeed.

It's so quiet
I can hear myself step in the leaves
I can hear myself think
I can hear trees whisper
It's so dark I can't see
It's so dark I can see eyes glow in front of me
And it's dark, very dark indeed.

Maneesh Sharma (8)
St Christopher's Preparatory School, Wembley

COLOURS

The colour red spreads your eyes
with grumpiness and sadness
The colour yellow brightens your eyes
with joy and laughter
The colour orange brings your eyes
both joy and sadness
The colour green widens your eyes
with happiness and scenery
The colour violet makes you dream
Are you going to win?

Aisha Natamkar (8)
St Christopher's Preparatory School, Wembley

IMAGINATION

I'm imagining this lonely field covered with snow
Just like the blank page in front of me
But something else is out there
Something else is coming.

I look around the room, nothing
But something is moving
Something is coming from dark into light
It's entering the wilderness.

Gracefully, cautiously as a ballerina
A deer's nose pokes out of a bush
It blinks, then it comes closer
It's coming more and more and more.

Prints darting about in the snow
In and out of trees
Its shadow springing all over the field
Of an animal that is sure to come.

Dark eyes blink at me
The deep green of its eyes
Amazingly, perfectly shaped
Looking warily, looking sad.

A sudden movement of a body
It enters the forest ahead
The room is still empty, the fire blazing
The page is full.

Anna Lunson (11)
St Stephen's Junior School, St Margarets

IT'S ONLY A GAME

It was a summer morning,
When awoken by a cry
Of seventeen mad horses,
Galloping towards the sky.

The mud flew on their faces
As they trotted with such speed
And their eyes had all glazed over,
As they ran right past Moormead.

They didn't stop for grass,
Not even for horseshoes,
But they cantered through The Turks Head,
Spilling all the booze.

Now there was a clever chap
Who put a gun before their eyes,
It's a shame the story goes like this,
But the old fella dies.

The horses trampled recklessly
Upon our fellow friend,
With all the blood and all the bones,
It was a pretty gory end.

The little creatures grunted
Up to this very day,
Until I reached out with my giant hand
And took them right away!

Emma Walker (11)
St Stephen's Junior School, St Margarets

THE ELEMENTS OF LIFE

Earth, wind, fire and water, four precious gifts of life.
The air sings a song of love, fire warms up the heart.
Earth, it provides us with flowers of beauty,
Water produces sea creatures full of life.

All of these things are precious but I give it all up
For the special people in my life.
I give it all up for the people I love
As I've got to spell it out *luv!*

The flowers, the trees, all the beauties of the world,
The things I love to see so much
As they grow even taller

Spread sunshine across the land,
I give it up for the things I love
From the heart of mankind and love.

Earth, wind, fire and water, four precious gifts of life.
The air sings a song of love, fire warms up the heart.
Earth, it provides us with flowers of beauty,
Water produces sea creatures full of life!

Nathan Kenneth King (9)
St Stephen's Junior School, St Margarets

TIMMY

Bright twinkly eyes staring through the bars
Those tiny feet scurrying around the wheel
A funny smile on his face
His ginger back standing out
Like a fire in the dark.

A snuffly nose at the end of his chubby face
Tickly whiskers brushing across my hand
His stubby tail wagging here and there
That squeaky wheel waking me up
Oh how I wish I had a hamster!

Henry Herbert (8)
St Stephen's Junior School, St Margarets

HOMEWORK

Homework, oh homework, I hate you, you smell,
I wish I could send you straight down to Hell.

The teacher is mad, I cannot believe,
I think they are trying to make me leave.

The annoying thing is, that if your homework comes in late,
you have to stay in during break.

The teacher is driving me insane,
attempting to look for my brain.

Of course it's there, they cannot see
that I am as clever as can be!

It's just that I would rather play,
than studying hard at the end of the day.

The homework today is all about flowers
and it will take me hours and hours.

Tomorrow a new day will start,
we are doing a play, I got the main part!

Harriet Roberts (9)
St Stephen's Junior School, St Margarets

SCHOOL TESTS

School tests are ever so boring,
Especially when the rain is pouring,
A grey day
As we sit in dismay
Trying to work out the sums.

School tests are *gruesome* and *frightening,*
Ah ha, there's the answer - lightning!
I bang the table, I bang my head
Trying to work out what the question said.

The test is over,
The day is done,
Now we rush home
To see our mum!

Iona Jackson (8)
St Stephen's Junior School, St Margarets

WEEPING WILLOW

Weeping willow do not fret
For you have nothing to regret.
Life is short and life is sweet,
To live life is a great feat.

Time is wasted every day.
So please don't let it slip away.
Don't be afraid to do a deed
And help someone in time of need.

Life is good and life is great,
You can do nothing to stop fate.

Jack Davis (11)
St Stephen's Junior School, St Margarets

A Special Person In My Life - My Grandad

He's very tall and thin
With a hairy, scratchy beard.
He crouches a little bit
When he stands and walks.
His eyebrows are thick
And grey like his hair.

On Saturdays, Sundays and Wednesdays
He always goes gliding.
Watercolour painting
Is another of his hobbies.
Every day Grandad walks to the shops
To buy a newspaper and later do the crossword.
If he has any spare time
He plays his musical instruments.
He's a great grandad to have.

Alice Hollyer (9)
St Stephen's Junior School, St Margarets

The Pear Tree

It sits in the garden all day
Never to move or never to sway.
The pears on it grow and die
Never to be picked, I wonder why.
Then one day a bird flew overhead,
Never had food or never had been fed.
It swooped down and picked at a pear,
Swoosh, swoosh
And then it was gone there and then
Never to be seen again!

Millie Driver (10)
St Stephen's Junior School, St Margarets

SNOW

Last weekend it snowed.
When we woke up
Everything was silent.

Then the ducks on the river
Started quacking.
The bells in the church
Were chiming.
Old ladies fell down
And cried.
Children threw snowballs
And shouted in the playground.
Cars slid on the road
And crashed.
Boats in the harbour
Sounded their horns.

But the snow
Fell very quietly.

Jeremy Freeman (8)
St Stephen's Junior School, St Margarets

SNOW

I like snow when it's crisp and white,
Smooth and clean and extremely bright.
That is when it has only just snowed,
When the twinkling crystals glow.
I look out the window, it is all rich and grand,
I watch the snowflakes expand and expand.
I say to myself, I must get out, I must get out,
Then I start rushing about.
At last, when I find my wellies,
I run out the door and see my friend, Kelly.

She grins and says, 'Do you want a snowball fight?'
I prepare my snowball and throw with all my might.
Kelly and I have so much fun,
But too soon I'm called in by my mum.
Kelly and I make plans for tomorrow,
But much to my sorrow,
When I wake up next day,
The snow has all melted away.

Jennie Baker-Dragun (8)
St Stephen's Junior School, St Margarets

MONKEY

My friend lives in the jungle,
He swings from tree to tree.
He has hair all over his body,
Just like me!

My friend wears a little hat,
It's quite a dirty brown.
He also has a tail
For hanging upside down.

People think I'm silly
When I hold monkey in my hand.
But he's my smallest friend
And . . .

I love him!

Alastair Freeman (8)
St Stephen's Junior School, St Margarets

ON MY SLED

The snow was still there when I came home from school,
I dressed to keep warm but tried to look cool.

I dashed to the shed to get out my sled,
We jumped in the car and off we all sped.

We got to the park before it got dark,
Like Jack and Jill we went up the hill.

I jumped upon my noble steed and started slowly to gather speed,
I went over a bump and landed with a thump.

But I stayed on my sled then went thud in the mud,
I did the longest slide, you should have seen me glide.

We all had a last go, said goodbye to the snow,
We went home for tea and put the sled in the shed,
Then I crawled up the stairs and fell into bed.

Will Latter (9)
St Stephen's Junior School, St Margarets

THE GALE

Lightning whipped the tar-black sky
And cackled at the thunder.
The flooded streets looked up to see
The fierce ice-cold rain.
Wind was racing through the clouds
And whistled at the windowpane.
Next he blew away the blue.
Thunder rolled around the heavens
Playing on his drum,
Then lightning came back for more as if to say,
'You've had your turn.'

Lottie Herbert (10)
St Stephen's Junior School, St Margarets

WHY ARE WE?

Why are we?

Why are some of us evil?
Why are some of us good?
And who made up the story
Of the little girl and her hood?

And if man made the word
Which was, of course, 'Hello,'
Is that how everything started
So many years ago?

Who are the people we follow?
Who are the people who lead?
And how do we remember
Who did a brilliant deed?

Who made the padlock,
Or more importantly . . . who made the key?
And why?
Why are we?

Rosie Beard (11)
St Stephen's Junior School, St Margarets

THE FIRST DAY OF SPRING

The daffodils open up like the jaws of a crocodile.
Newborn bunnies bounce about on pogo sticks.
The lambs stumble their first step.
The fruits are so juicy they burst into small delicious pieces of fruit.
The corn shoots up to reach the sky getting ready for the harvest.
The spring bubbles and overflows watering the crops.

Ben Lawrence (9)
St Stephen's Junior School, St Margarets

WAITING

I'm sitting here,
on my chair,
waiting for my mum to cut my pear,
my crunchy, juicy pear.

And while I'm waiting, I am watching a blackbird pecking on the lawn.

I'm sitting here,
near my plate,
waiting for my next pancake,
my golden, tempting pancake.

And while I'm waiting, I am reading the toy mail order catalogue.

I'm sitting here,
in my place,
waiting for snail to win the race,
my slowly moving snail.

And while I'm waiting, I am gazing at the clouds gliding past above.

I'm sitting here
with my pet,
waiting for the sun to set,
the orange-yellow sun.

And while I'm waiting, I am drawing dolphins leaping high in the sea.

I'm waiting here,
waiting to grow up.
The good times and the bad,

and while I'm waiting,
I am hoping,
fearing,
laughing,
crying
and travelling the long journey of childhood.

Waiting, waiting, waiting, waiting, waiting . . .

Katy Backler (8)
St Stephen's Junior School, St Margarets

THE SNOW JAM

Slow, sticky in the snow,
When will I get there? I don't know,
I've been sitting here for hours and hours,
The lorries in front are as big as towers.

The snow plough would make a quicker way,
I wish there was one here today,
My car is just a small MG,
So getting there is not to be.

I've wrapped a blanket round my knees,
My tiny hands will start to freeze,
It's so gloomy, it's like night,
I really need a bit of light.

What's this, another lorry now?
But no, it is a big snow plough!
So very soon I'll be away
From this old boring motorway.

William McDermott (9)
St Stephen's Junior School, St Margarets

PETER CRUTCH

I was ever so sorry to see you go,
Whether your death was fast or slow,
You were the same lovely, old you,
To all of us through and through.

You might have had cold feet,
Or toasty, warm hands,
It makes no difference,
You were still the same man.

It may be quite dull,
Or lonely without you,
But at least your heart
Was loved, warm and true.

You warmed up my day,
When quite close to tears,
You helped me overcome
My worries and fears.

I loved you so much,
It was hardly true,
Your touch so gentle,
But I knew it was you.

The poem could go on
About the good things you did,
But what David explained,
A naughty young kid.

I guess it ends here,
My poem, I mean,
Not our relationship,
That can go on in our *dreams!*

Anabelle Callaway (11)
St Stephen's Junior School, St Margarets

MY GRANDPA

My grandpa is ill but still
He looks in the mirror
thinking he's a model.
He thinks his hair is cool
though he hardly has any.
He likes to play golf every day
but never comes first.
He thinks he's a tennis pro
but keeps serving into the net.
He always hides from me when I visit
but I always know where he is.
Grandpa thinks he's Will Young
but sounds like a cat getting strangled.
My grandpa is very special indeed!

James Ball (9)
St Stephen's Junior School, St Margarets

MY COUSIN

Talk, talk, talk
All about sport.
Check, check, check,
Always playing chess.
Bleep, bleep, bleep,
Good at computer games.
Fuss, fuss, fuss,
Such a picky eater.
Giggle, giggle, giggle,
Has his crazy moments!

Joanna Yale (9)
St Stephen's Junior School, St Margarets

MY CAT

Its eyes like sparkling green emeralds
Shining in the dead of night,
Its tail as wiggly as a snake
Slithering through the tall elephant grass,
Fur like thick black velvet
Being sewn into a lady's dress,
Paws as white as snowflakes
Falling from a winter sky
And a nose the pink of a ballerina's tutu
Floating across the stage.
My cat is always dozing
Like a sleeping baby,
Chasing string
Like a bear with a fish,
Or looking to be stroked,
A passenger waiting for a bus.
He's the one who makes me happy,
He's like one big summer holiday.

My cat.

Scarlett Young (8)
St Stephen's Junior School, St Margarets

WINTER

Tall, bare trees like spilt black ink spreading out in all directions,
Crystal twinkling snow blanketing the ground like a thick duvet,
Crackling orange fires glowing like the huge burning sun,
And beautifully decorated Christmas trees standing grandly
like smartly dressed soldiers.

Georgia Skinner (8)
St Stephen's Junior School, St Margarets

THE FIRESIDE

The fire is like orange and red birds fluttering as they learn to fly.
The coal looks like burnt muffins being pecked away by
                                     the hungry birds.
It sounds like fireworks shooting into the sky.
It feels like the rays of the sun are trying to burn your skin.
The piece of wood leaning over the coal looks like a cheetah
Ready to catch its prey.
The coal scuttle looks like a wide mouth ready to eat the burnt muffins.
The smoke looks like magic rising up into space,
It is like a huge bee buzzing about.
The mantelpiece is like a long piece of bark
Waiting to have its leaves back on.
I like the fire because it keeps me warm and cosy.

Toby Piachaud (9)
St Stephen's Junior School, St Margarets

THE BEE

This morning my teacher said to me,
'Write a poem about a bee.'
I thought this through, proper and right,
Then I thought, what shall I write?
I'll start with the body, all yellow and black,
Then move onto the wings stuck to its back.
It has six legs all bent and funny
And it uses its nose to burrow for honey.
When it sees a flower, it dives to the scene
And collects all the pollen to give to the queen.

Grace Cooper (9)
St Stephen's Junior School, St Margarets

LIGHT

Orangey-yellow, bluey-white,
Flickering light in the dark of night.
Birthdays and parties, churches and a hall,
A candle is very important for them all.
When it gets blown it will rapidly flicker,
When it's your birthday it makes you a wisher.
It's my friend for reading late at night,
Providing me with lots of light.
Hanging in lanterns placed by the stair,
Burning smells filling the air.
After a while the wax will melt,
In an instant the smoke is smelt.

Thomas Alington (9)
St Stephen's Junior School, St Margarets

GOING TO SCHOOL

Going to school is so boring,
I'd much prefer to do some drawing.
Sitting there with my back to the wall,
I really do not like going to school.

The next day my teacher said,
'Write a poem about a bed,'
So I just sat there on my own,
Not even caring if I'm all alone.

I'm always daydreaming off to space
And flying until I'm green in the face.

Eve Edmunds (9)
St Stephen's Junior School, St Margarets

ONE DAY THAT COULD BE YOU

If you see an old man walking down the street,
Don't just walk right past him,
Look at his feet,
If he's wearing leather shoes that are shiny and new,
Say hello and walk on by,
There's nothing you can do,
But if he's wearing no shoes and looking sad and blue,
Try and lend a hand because . . .
One day that could be you.

Harvey Bassett (8)
St Stephen's Junior School, St Margarets

ROCK POOLING

I carefully leap from rock to rock
Full of excitement for the treasures
I am going to find.
I plunge my hand into the nearest rock pool,
I see an orange starfish
Among the fingers of seaweed.
Suddenly, I see a shrimp dart under a rock,
The water ripples as it disappears.
I can feel the wind blowing through my hair
And the hot sun on the back of my neck.
I balance my bucket on a rock
As I swish my net into the water
And catch the shrimp.

Anna Smethurst (9)
St Stephen's Junior School, St Margarets

MY FRIEND SID

Day 1

Boring as the supermarket where you shop at town,
Funny as a squawking parrot who's acting like a clown.

Day 2

Amusing as a madman who's lying on the streets,
Muddy as a hairy boar eating loads of beets.

Day 3

Sticky as a glue stick in my pencil case,
Scary as a ghost that haunts a long staircase.

Day 4

Tall as an old oak tree that's been there for years,
Hurt as a fallen toddler who's just about in tears.

Day 5

Jumpy as a hopping rabbit that's about to be gunned down,
Mad as a barking collie that's caged up in a pound.

Day 6

Peaceful as a band of hippies in a caravan,
Sporty as David Beckham plus he has loads of fans.

Day 7

Healthy as a piece of cabbage, *yuck!* We don't like that,
Crazy as a mad hatter who wears a tall top hat.

Day 8

Old as a feeble grandad who's still telling stories,
Exciting as Lord Of The Rings, but (luckily) it's gory.

Day 9

Wet as a farmer who's been out in the rain,
Bonkers as a brown Alsatian that's just gone insane.

Day 10

Fit as a wrestler who'll kill you in the ring,
Demanding as a football coach who'll shout, 'Get on the wing!'

Day 11

Rich as the royal family, rolling in glory they are,
Drunk as a wobbly boozer who'll spend all night in a bar.

Day 12

Stout as a dwarf who's in fairy tales,
Sad as a loser who always fails.

Day 13

Sleepy as a sloth in the rainforest,
Skint as a peasant who really is the poorest.

Day 14

Childish as a grown-up who's acting like a kid,
Motionless as a dead body, that's my friend, Sid!

Christy Born (9)
St Stephen's Junior School, St Margarets

THINGS THAT GO BUMP IN THE NIGHT!

While you're tucked up fast asleep,
Out from the corners
Strange shadows creep.
Shadows of witches, shadows of ghosts,
Out from the letterbox strange things post.

So try not to worry, don't take fright,
When things go bump in the night!

Ghosts glide in your room,
Sneak under your bed
And pull at the pillows
Where you rest your sleepy head.

So try not to worry, don't take fright,
When things go bump in the night!

Ghosts glide down the hallway,
Wall through wall,
You can't make out the pictures because the shadows are so tall.

Spooks tweak at your toes
And use white feathers to tickle your nose.

So try not to worry, don't take fright,
When things go bump in the night!

Sleep tight!

Saba Aurangzaib (11)
Tudor Primary School

MY NIGHTMARE

My nightmare was very bad,
I started to go really mad!
I saw a fat, ugly witch,
She began to itch!

The monsters were making a racket
In the attic!
I started to panic, I didn't know what to do,
I needed to go to the loo.
That's when I woke up
And saw a weird looking cup!

Pooja Bhatti (10)
Tudor Primary School

SISTERS ARE GREAT

Sisters are great,
She's always your mate.
She loves to play,
All day.
She is kind,
But she is always behind.
Who will I play with if she is not there?
Who will be my friend?
Well, I've got a sister,
Hey, Mister,
Don't mess with my sister!
What would I do without a sister like her?
She is great
And she is never late.
Sometimes she is scared,
But she's never feared.
She is like a mouse in the corner,
Sitting there silently.
She hides behind the door,
While I sleep on the floor.
When I'm in trouble
She's always there to help me,
I have a kind and caring sister!

Sukhveer Kaur Grewal (10)
Tudor Primary School

HULLABALOO

Hullabaloo, hullabaloo, everyone caused a hullabaloo!
The chickens, the cows, the pigs, the dogs
They all caused a hullabaloo.
Hullabaloo, hullabaloo, everyone caused a hullabaloo!

The chickens did a poo
And they all caused a hullabaloo.
The cows all did a deafening moo
And they all caused a hullabaloo.
The pigs used the grubby loo
And they all caused a hullabaloo.
The dogs made a vile stew
And they all caused a hullabaloo.

The chickens, the cows, the pigs, the dogs
They all caused a hullabaloo.
Hullabaloo! Hullabaloo! They all caused a hullabaloo!
Hullabaloo! Hullabaloo! Do you know how to cause a hullabaloo?

Rameeta Bhamra (11)
Tudor Primary School

A HOT TIME IN THE SUPERMARKET

When my mum gave my dad
The juiciest, most romantic kiss
Right there in the supermarket
And worse began to quickstep him down the aisle
To their favourite tune,
I couldn't believe it,
Everybody stared,
My cheeks began to burn.

Sukhdeep Sandhu (10)
Tudor Primary School

HEARTBREAKER

I fell in love
But I got a broken heart,
He left me and went to Spain
And that made us part.

He's the only one I've ever loved,
He left and went away.
I really thought we hit it off,
I really wanted him to stay.

Well bad luck for me, now he's gone,
I loved him more than ever.
My love for him will never fade,
I will love him forever.

Heartbreaker!

Orkid Catherine Wildman (11)
Tudor Primary School

CHRISTMAS

C   is for Claus.
H   is for happy.
R   is for reindeer.
I   is for ice.
S   is for Santa.
T   is for tree.
M is for magical.
A   is for antlers.
S   is for snow.

That's what Christmas is all about!

Charanpal Bhangal (11)
Tudor Primary School

WRESTLERS

Wow, he is so weak
Or am I thick like an ant?
He might be strong
Or am I wrong?
I don't know, I don't have time to think
Or he might get his strength back.

What's he doing? Why ain't he beating me?
Is Kane going to forfeit?
Well, this is my only chance,
If only I could find the belt,
It is easy to beat him,
I might be the heavy weight champion.

Oh no, he's coming near me,
Kane's going to do a chokeslam
But I was wrong,
I said, 'We both forfeit,
Let's skip out of this mess!

Paveen Thiruganam (10)
Tudor Primary School

MY POEM

Love is a nice way to start the day,
It makes you get out of bed.
Love is what throws open your curtains
And somersaults on your head.

Love is warm and cosy,
You get it when you cuddle up to your mum
And love is a feeling of laughing out loud
When somebody tickles your tum.

Love is a pleasant thing
And love's making friends with the bees.
Even the flowers are bursting with love
When they are dancing in the breeze.

Saima Wazir (10)
Tudor Primary School

WHAT PARENTS WEAR IN BED

Can anyone guess
What parents wear in bed?
We held a little club
To see what parents said.

We made a little chart
Though parents wouldn't say,
But it's surely something funny
As they turn grey.

Tina's mum is quite modern,
She wears a mini skirt.
Rina's dad is old-fashioned,
He wears a ragged shirt.

Garry's mum is an old singer
So she wears a heavy dress.
Harry's dad wears a nappy suit
Because he makes a lot of mess.

Eric's dad is a show-off
So he wears some fancy pants.
Deric's mum wears her nightie,
Above it are some ants.

Ramandeep Kaur Walia (10)
Tudor Primary School

MY DREAM

Last night I had a dream,
It was as weird as it seemed.
I was flying so high,
I flew into the sky.
Suddenly I was going to crash,
Then I landed with a bash.
Weird, I wasn't home,
For in fact I was in Rome.
Then these two men took me away
And I didn't want to stay.
Then I saw next to the juice squeezer,
Sitting down was Julius Caesar.
A man shouted, 'Here's a boy, I picked him.'
But now I had to be the victim.
Caesar said, 'What's your name? Is it Brian.
Oh whatever, release the lion!'
I ran for my life, I ran,
I ran as fast as I can.
Then I woke up, it was a dream,
It was as weird as it seemed.

Ricky Sultani (11)
Tudor Primary School

UNTITLED

Look at the bangle
On my wrist,
See it shine from every angle.
Watch it dangle
From my wrist
And hear it jingle-jangle!

Ketan Bhardwa (9)
Tudor Primary School

HELL OR HEAVEN?

I just escaped from the likes of Hell,
I ran and ran till I saw the sight of Heaven,
The blazing light blazed before my eyes
And banished my weeping sorrows,
But in my guilty conscience I trembled
Beneath within my soul,
Thinking of the damage I caused.
I crept away from this lie,
Fearing that the Devil didn't hear my cry.
'Please don't hurt me,' I whispered to myself,
My guilty conscience fought for me,
It took over my body,
It took over my soul,
That was the end for poor old Koul.

Sher Singh Sandhu (10)
Tudor Primary School

I SAW A PEACOCK

I saw a peacock with a fairy tail,
I saw a shark fall on a snail,
I saw a cloud all wrapped around with ivy,
I saw a dog on a muddy ground.

I saw a beetle swallow up a whale,
I saw a man with incredible nails,
I saw a house as high as the moon,
I saw wet eyes in flames of a living fire.

I saw a peacock with a fairy tail,
I saw a shark fall on a snail,
I saw a cloud all wrapped around with ivy,
I saw a dog on a muddy ground.

Maninder Singh Sahota (10)
Tudor Primary School

A Little Spooky Limerick

There is a well
That has a gold bell,
It's on the tower,
It has power
And it fell . . .

Manpreet Aujla (8)
Tudor Primary School

Book Crook

Once there was a man,
He bought a fan.
There was a crook,
He looked in a book
And he drinks from a can.

Reema Beghi (8)
Tudor Primary School

The Stool

I saw a stool
Next to the pool.
Then he started to call,
'I want that ball!'
Then he thought he was cool.

Jaya Singh (8)
Tudor Primary School

POETRY MAYHEM

Mrs Prance,
    The one who taught us to dance,
Was always near a circumstance.
If she was eaten
And I was beaten,
We were always comfortably seaten.

Mrs Bitter,
    She was a brilliant knitter,
I was into tidying litter,
She said, 'No,'
And I said, 'So,'
But she knew that I was a really good hitter.

Mrs Prickers,
    She's always giving us stickers,
Was usually moody
But certainly rudey.
She made us laugh, by drawing a graph,
Which showed her favourite, chocolate Snickers.

Then there was Gran,
Who mostly ate a lot of bran,
Was always bringing her golden pan
In an enormously multicoloured van.

And that was our little poem,
Of all the mayhem,
Which made us giggle
And certainly wiggle.

Gurjit Bir (11) & Jasmine Bir (8)
Tudor Primary School

OLD POLLY

Old Polly found a frog,
She didn't like it so she swapped it for a dog,
The dog didn't bark
So she swapped it for a shark,
The shark looked savage
So she swapped it for a cabbage,
The cabbage was too big
So she swapped it for a pig,
The pig was too bony
So she swapped it for a pony,
The pony wouldn't trot
So she swapped it for a pot,
The pot wouldn't cook
So she swapped it for a book,
But the book had no pictures
So she swapped it all for nothing.

Dhruval Patel (11)
Tudor Primary School

MY OWN LIMERICK

A little girl who had long hair
Left her earring on the table then was bare.
There was a winner,
His name was Rumplestiltskin and he was a spinner.
The girl came near and near.

Zarmila Thararchayan (8)
Tudor Primary School